W.I.N. 2:
Insights Into Training and Leading Warriors

Edited by Brian R. Willis

Warrior Spirit Books
A Division of Winning Mind Training Inc.
Calgary, Alberta

Library and Archives Canada Cataloguing in Publication

W.I.N. 2: Insights into Training and Leading Warriors / editor: Brian R. Willis

ISBN 978-0-9808819-1-2

1. Police training. I. Willis, Brian R.

HV7923.W553 2009   363.2   C2009-900604-9

© 2009 by Brian R. Willis

ISBN 978-0-9808819-1-2

All rights reserved. Except for use in a review, no portion of this book may be reproduced in any form without the expressed written permission of the publisher.

Publisher:
Warrior Spirit Books
A Division of Winning Mind Training Inc.
396 Sienna Park Drive S.W.
Calgary, Alberta T3H 3K3 Canada
www.warriorspiritbooks.com

Design and Production:
Nadien Cole Advertising, Calgary, Alberta

Project Management: Debbie Elicksen, Freelance Communications, Calgary, Alberta

Cover Photograph: Mike Starchuk

W.I.N. 2: Insights into Training and Leading Warriors—First Edition
Printed and bound in the United States
Copyright 2009

Table of Contents

Foreword by Lt. Col. Dave Grossman 6

Acknowledgements 9

Preface 11

1. **Warrior Spirit**
   One Warrior's Creed, A Philosophy
   to Live With by Randy Watt 19

   Good Vs Evil: A Story About Winning
   by Marcus Young 25

   Tactical Mindset by Massad Ayoob 34

   Cultivating the Warrior Spirit
   by Sgt. Gregg W. Gaby 39

   Stay Dangerous by George Demetriou 44

2. **Training to Win**
   Training to Win by Brian Willis 57

   Training the Gutterfighter Way
   by Steven Mosley 65

   Training for the Real Fight by Paul Howe 71

   Tired of Feel Good Training? Challenge
   Yourself by Henk Iverson 79

   Training Issues – As I See It by Kelly Keith 88

   Fit for Duty? by James Di Naso 96

3. **Warrior Reflections**
   The Elephant in the Corner by Jeff Baker 105

The Survival Triangle by Alexis Artwohl, PhD 111

The C-Zone of Combat Preparation
by Harvey V. Hedden 120

Ambiguous Rules of Engagement and the
Fallacy of the Green Light by Brian K. Sain. 131

The Adventure of Foreign Policing Missions
by David S. Butzer 149

4. Training Insights
Training Gaps by Brian Willis 163

Degrees of Police Training by Mike Starchuk 174

Plan to Train, or Plan to Fail by Steven D. Ashley 181

Training Officers in the Reasonable Employment
of the Knife by George T. Williams. 194

The Slaughter of Innocents. Understanding the
Five Phases of the Active Shooter by Dan Marcou 209

A Discussion of the Importance of a Holistic
Approach to the Training of Attitudes and Mental
Preparedness in Police Officers by Jim Dowle 221

12 Tips to Implement. A New Paradigm in Your
Defensive Tactics Program by Tom Gillis 238

Forging A Warrior's Mettle by Ron Borsch 249

5. After the Fight
The Art of Articulation by Brian Willis
and Darren Leggatt 263

Incomplete Officer Survival: The Importance
of Self-Aid Training by Eric Dickinson 278

Enemy at the Gate by Martin Smith 288

Officer Training: Defending Your Actions in
Civil Rights Litigation by Laura L. Scarry 299

Using Forensic Equipment to Enhance Use
of Force Investigations by Curtis J. (Jeff) Cope
and Kim Swobodzinski 307

Foreword

by
Lt. Col. Dave Grossman

This is a vitally important collection of writing by some of the great warriors and great minds of our age.

We are in the midst of what I have termed the Warrior Renaissance...an explosion of knowledge and understanding in a vital field of human endeavor. Indeed, in the last 50 years we have learned more about the physiology and psychology of combat, human aggression, fear, and the needs and responses of humans to stress and challenge, than in the previous 5,000 years put together. Bruce Siddle has termed this 'warrior science' and Tony Blauer calls it 'the Golden Age of Warriors.'

And the warriors in this collection, every single one of them, are true leaders, giants in the land; trail blazers, contributors and chroniclers for this Renaissance, this explosion of knowledge.

In most cases these warriors have been in combat. They have "seen the elephant"...they have gone into the heart of darkness and returned to tell their tales; and if they believe that these lessons are of value, if they think that having known these lessons ahead of time would have helped them, then there must be no doubt in our minds that we should study and learn from these narratives.

For we are living in stunningly violent times...

Medical technology saves ever more lives, preventing ever more murders every year, but the rate at which our citizens are trying to kill each other is the highest in recorded peacetime history. A study conducted by the University of Massachusetts and Harvard University in 2002 demonstrated that if we had 1970's level medical technology today, the murder rate would be nearly four time what it is. In other words, the advances in medical technology today prevent three out of four murders.

If we had 1930's level technology (no automobiles or telephones for most people, and no antibiotics) the murder rate would probably be at least 10 times what it is today.

If we had 1870's frontier-level medical technology (no cars, no phones, no antibiotics, no antiseptics, and no anesthesia) the murder rate would probably be 15 times what it is now. Thus we live in times that make the violence of the Old West pale by comparison. This explosion of the serious assault rate is true in every major industrialized nation around the world.

Additionally, in the post-9/11 world, we are faced with a great external challenge to our nation, our way of life, and our civilization.

Now, more than ever, we must capture the wisdom of these warrior-leader-trainers.

You can think of this book as 'The Book of Virtues' for warriors. You hold in your hands a vital resource for all warriors who desire to understand and contribute to the great challenge of this age. Yet, in one very important way, this book is nothing new. This book, and these writers are a new chapter in a long line of heroes... warriors who personify the values that made our nations great...and still can! As J.R.R. Tolkien put it, in The Lord of the Rings,

> Not all that is gold doth glitter,
> Not all those who wander are lost.
> The old that is strong does not whither,
> and the deep roots are not touched by the frost.

Now, in this dark hour, let us tap the strength that is drawn from the roots of our warrior-heritage, deep roots that have endured the bitter frost. Let us learn the new while still seeking out the old that is strong and does not whither, in order to answer the challenge of the age.

So don't just read this book: study it, apply it, and pass it on to the next generation. Pass on the flame! "For this shall the good man teach his son," that future generations of warriors may be sustained and inspired.

Dave Grossman
Lt. Colonel, U.S. Army (ret.)
Author, On Killing and On Combat
www.killology.com

Acknowledgements

Many people have influenced me throughout my law enforcement career. Many more have influenced me as a trainer. It would be impossible to acknowledge all of those people. I must however take time to acknowledge some of them.

First and foremost I want to thank all the warrior leaders and trainers who made the time to contribute and support this project. Their efforts and writings are greatly appreciated. Without their commitment this book would not have become a reality.

I owe a great deal to the past and present members of the Calgary Police Skills and Procedures Unit. This group of warrior trainers and warrior leaders continue to inspire, tolerate, teach, and support me. They have impacted me as a law enforcement officer, a trainer, a teacher, a leader, a learner and a person.

I want to thank Ed Nowicki, Dianne Nowicki, Gena Nowicki, Harvey Hedden, Steve Ashley, Jim Smith and the countless others who give tirelessly to make ILEETA (the International Law Enforcement Educators and Trainers Association) the premiere law enforcement training organization in the world. ILEETA has and will continue to save officers lives by positively influencing law enforcement training around the world. It is impossible to measure the number of lives that have been saved and influenced through the efforts of these great people. On behalf of myself and all law enforcement officers, thank you.

Special thanks to Mark (Sponge) Zbojniewicz for his tireless efforts, guidance and support with this book. As with the first book, W.I.N. Critical Issues in Training and Leading Warriors, Sponge has put in countless hours to help make this project a reality and I am grateful for his patience, guidance and friendship.

This ackowledgement would not be complete without special thanks to my wife Lynda, my sons Jesse and Cody and my family for the important role they have played. It is their unconditional love, support, advice, role modeling and direction that has helped to mold my career and untimately this project. My wish is that the information in this book provides officers with tools to help them go home to their family every day.

Preface

W.I.N. – An acronym for 'Life's Most Powerful Question' – What's Important Now?

Every day, in their personal and professional lives, warriors are faced with a number of choices and decisions – some more critical than others. The decisions they make in response to those choices have a lasting impact on their health, relationships, finances, careers and ultimately their safety.

Warriors in law enforcement, corrections and the military face a unique and exciting blend of opportunities and challenges. This book is a collection of insights, philosophies, stories and thoughts that reflect What's Important Now in relation to training and leading today's warriors. In putting together this powerful book I have sought input from warrior trainers and warrior leaders from Canada, the United States and the United Kingdom. I have the honor of knowing many of them personally and others I know by reputation. All of them were willing to make time in their hectic lives to put their thoughts and insights on paper so they could be shared with others. Their motive to improve training, inspire leaders, and save lives was completely selfless.

What's Important Now?

This one powerful question allows us to prioritize decisions, choices, actions, and events in our personal and professional lives. The reason this is such a powerful question is that although it is about the present it has a powerful impact on the future. The simple act of asking this question causes the warrior's mind to almost instantly imagine the impact of the choices he or she are faced with and quickly identify the most desirable one. I do not mean the choice that will provide the most immediate gratification. Instead, I mean the choice that will have the most positive impact in the warrior's life based on the foreseeable future.

Eleanor Roosevelt had this to say about the importance of choices:

> "One's philosophy is not best expressed in words; it is expressed in the choices one makes. In thelong run, we shape our lives and we shape ourselves. The process never ends until we die. And the choices we make are ultimately our own responsibility."

The choices warriors face every day can vary greatly in difficulty and long-term implications.

Some should be relatively easy:

- Large or extra large coffee?
- Room for cream in your coffee?
- Regular or premium gas?
- Do you make a healthy selection from the menu at the restaurant or do you make the unhealthy choice that you know you will regret later?
- Does this tie go with this shirt?
- White or red wine with your meal?
- Do you drive home after 'a few drinks' or do you ask for a ride or take a cab?

Some get at the true core of: What's important to you in life:

- Do you spend an hour on the couch watching mindless television or do you spend that time in a personal development activity such as working out or reading? (One hour of reading a day equates to 364 hours or, said another way, nine 40 hour weeks of learning per year. That equates to 9,100 hours over a 25 year career.)

- Do you listen to the radio in your vehicle while commuting or do you use the time to listen to educational and motivational CD's? (For the average person this is another opportunity for 364 hours of learning a year.)

- Do you, once again, go for a drink with the people from work at the end of the day or do you go home and spend time with your family?

- Do you take the opportunity to praise the good work and effort of co-workers or do you take credit for their work?

- Do you celebrate the successes in your life or do you focus on the failures?

- Do you do what is right or what is popular?

- Do you do what is right or what is expedient?

- Do you celebrate the strengths of your children and your significant other or do you focus on their mistakes and weaknesses?

- Do you focus on the strengths and talents of your co-workers and your subordinates or do you focus on their weaknesses and failures?

- Do you bring up a colleague's mistake, which was made in front of everyone at a meeting to embarrass him or her, or do you address it in private to draw out the learning points from the experience?

- Do you take responsibility for your actions and decisions or do you look for someone and something to blame?

Others are more challenging and unique to the profession of law enforcement:

- Do you make 10 minutes a day to train your skills and tactics or do you only train when the department makes you? (10 minutes a day, 4 days a week, for 48 weeks a year equates to 32 hours of training a year.)

- Do you rush in to make the arrest, or assess, gather intelligence and wait until you have sufficient backup?

- Do you pursue, or use other means to apprehend the suspect?

- Do you terminate the pursuit or stay in it?

- Is this a foot chase or a foot-surveillance?

- Do you talk or do you fight?

- Do you know when it is time to walk away and when it is time to stay and fight?

- Do you close the gap and use empty hand control, or maintain distance and use an intermediate weapon?

- Do you shoot or not shoot?

As a warrior, what's important now, may change from minute to minute or second to second.

These decisions are the reason for the book. They are the reason that the contributors made the time to put their thoughts on paper so that others could learn from their knowledge, experience, successes and failures.

My hope for this volume, as with the previous volume: W.I.N. Critical Issues in Training and Leading Warriors is that officers will take the time to read and draw lessons from every chapter. You may not agree with what is written, and that is OK. My dream is that training academies and training organizations will use these volumes as textbooks for both new and experienced officers. Through these two volumes officers have the ability to learn from over 50 of the top trainers and leaders, and experience what few will get otherwise. The goal is not for these to be considered a 'bible' for training, but a text that challenges every one of us to evaluate our training, our interactions, our tactics and our lives to ensure that we are truly prepared to win.

Warrior Spirit

"A warrior is on permanent guard against the roughness of human behavior. A warrior is magical and ruthless, a maverick with the most refined taste and manners, whose worldly task is to sharpen, yet disguise, his cutting edge so that no one would be able to suspect his ruthlessness."

- The Power of Silence by Carlos Castaneda

THE "ONE WARRIOR'S CREED," A PHILOSOPHY TO LIVE WITH

by Randy Watt

One Warrior's Creed

If today is to be THE DAY, so be it. If you seek to do battle with me this day you will receive the best that I am capable of giving. It may not be enough, but it will be everything that I have to give and it will be impressive for I have constantly prepared myself for this day. I have trained, drilled and rehearsed my actions so that I might have the best chance of defeating you. I have kept myself in peak physical condition, schooled myself in the martial skills and have become proficient in the application of combat tactics. You may defeat me, but you will pay a severe price and will be lucky to escape with your life. You may kill me, but I am willing to die if necessary. I do not fear Death, for I have been close enough to it on enough occasions that it no longer concerns me. But I do fear the loss of my Honor and would rather die fighting than to have it said that I was without Courage. So I WILL FIGHT YOU, no matter how insurmountable it may seem, and to the death if need be, in order that it may never be said of me that I was not a Warrior.

© *Steven R. Watt, All Rights Reserved.*

I penned the creed during the closing days of my military tour in Iraq as a Counter-Terrorism Advisor to Iraqi Security Forces. I was reflecting on those I had known over my time in Special Forces and S.W.A.T., the truly dangerous and deadly men with whom I had shared fear, sweat and blood. Men committed to the cause of liberty, who believed that it was worth everything they had to give, even their lives. Men who exported their capability to far away places in the world where terror and tyranny reigned, and who, within the confines of the cities and jurisdictions within the greatest nation on earth, the United States of America, utilized their dedication and skill to protect the rights of those unable, or unwilling, to protect them for themselves. Men and women (for I personally know that courage is not limited to one gender) who truly represented the commitment to selfless service and willing sacrifice honed by previous generations of warriors.

I had been reflecting on a recent operation where a good friend had perished. He left behind a young family and numerous tears had been shed in the days following his death. At a memorial ceremony, words had been spoken, words that indicated the special nature of his service and it later caused me to wonder, "why do we do this?" Why do we, the "rough men" of whom Orwell speaks, voluntarily subject ourselves to the life-long efforts required to be the warriors, to become one of Dave Grossman's "sheepdogs"? As I reflected, I began to recognize some underlying values that were consistent among those of police and military special operations with whom I had served. The recognition of the constancy of those values resulted in the writing of "One Warrior's Creed," in an attempt to verbalize the values of the warriors of our great democracy.

If today is to be THE DAY, so be it. We do not know the day or the time when we will be called on and we do not care. By <u>living</u>, not just practicing, the creed, we will be ready no matter when or where. The day, time or place matters not. Stephanie Shugart, wife of MSG Randall Shugart, recipient of the Medal of Honor, said that "it takes a real man to live a creed, not just say it."

*If you seek to do battle with me...*we of the creed do not go looking for the fight, those purveying evil must bring it to us. We, the "quiet professionals," have nothing to demonstrate, nothing to show, no need to brag, we quietly go about our lives. We represent, as stated by the wife of one who lives the creed, "the most dangerous nice guy(s) you'll ever meet." But if you bring the battle to us, *you will receive the best that I am capable of giving.* We are committed to fighting you, to defending ourselves and those for whom we feel responsible, and we will give it our best effort no matter what.

*It may not be enough...*we recognize that we do not control the tactical environment enough to ensure the outcome...*but it will be everything that I have to give and it will be impressive, for I have constantly prepared myself for this day.* We recognize that the commitment and responsibility we took upon ourselves by oath requires that we put forth daily effort to ensure our skills are at their utmost when called for. *I have trained, drilled and rehearsed my actions so that I might have the best chance of defeating you.* Never knowing when, where or how, we accept the standard of being constantly ready. We daily sweat, strain and push ourselves far beyond the boundaries of mere mortals, then smile and prepare to do it again tomorrow. If the call to action never comes, we are okay with that, but we are not okay with the potential for failure due to a lack of preparation.

I have kept myself in peak physical condition... for a warrior not highly fit is less than half a warrior,... *schooled myself in the martial skills...* for we recognize that to be truly ready means that we must be capable of the use of the complete range of weapons, including firearms, blunt and edged weapons, personal weapons such as hands, elbows, knees and feet, and the mind,... *and have become proficient in the application of combat tactics.* We understand that, since we don't know where or when, we must understand the range of variables existing on any terrain and we must have prepared our strategies for fighting there.

You may defeat me... we know that we are mortal, we have no false illusions or ideas of being invulnerable, *but you will pay a severe price...* we will inflict upon you whatever pain and injury is necessary to insure your defeat, *and will be lucky to escape with your life...* we will take your life, without remorse, if you force us to do so. We do not enjoy killing, but we recognize that the taking of the life of an evil predator may be necessary in order to ensure the safety of ourselves, our loved ones, our cherished way of life and our nation.

You may kill me, but I am willing to die if necessary. We recognize that great sacrifices have been necessary in the past, in order to maintain the cause of freedom and to ensure a free society, and we honor those who have died in the cause of liberty. We also recognize that warriors must be willing to do so today and in the future, or the sacrifices of those who have paid the ultimate price in the past will become nothing more than a historical anecdote. *I do not fear death, for I have been close enough to it on enough occasions that it no longer concerns me.* We recognize that all who have received the God-given gift of mortality die, that it is nothing to be feared for it will come to us all. We do not get to choose the place or time of our demise, but we revel in the Roman proverb, "It is better to have lived one day as a lion than one hundred years as a sheep." We have been present when death has occurred and some of us have caused it. We have known warriors among us who have perished. We have honored them, paid tribute to the families who raised and supported them, and thanked God for the privilege of knowing them.

*But I do fear the loss of my Honor...*to live honorably is the root of our zeal, it provides the fuel for our efforts, which is why the word is capitalized. We, like the great warrior classes of old, recognize that a life without honor is a life wasted. We are committed to greater things than ourselves...*and would rather die fighting than to have it said that I was without Courage.* Courage is the exemplification of all that we hold in great value, of all that we feel is worth the ultimate price. To ever be without Courage is to truly be unarmed, unprepared, and easily overcome. We can never overstate its importance, which is why it is capitalized.

*So I WILL FIGHT YOU...*we strongly commit to that and exemplify it with how we live the creed...*no matter how insurmountable it may seem and to the death if need be.* We care not what the odds are or what the probable outcome may be. What is important is that we are there and ready...*in order that it may never be said of me that*

I was not a Warrior. To live in the shame of knowing that we capitulated, that we surrendered to fear, that we failed to exemplify the creed, that we have dishonored those before us, is a shame and humiliation beyond comprehension. That is the only thing the Warrior truly fears.

I hope that no sense of arrogance or conceit has pervaded this explanation, for that is not intended. My only desire is that the warriors among us may come to a better of understanding of who and what we are, so that we are strengthened in our commitment to live the "One Warrior's Creed."

Steven R. Watt (Randy) is an Assistant Chief of Police with the Ogden Police Department, Ogden, Utah, and is a Lieutenant Colonel in the 19th Special Forces Group, Utah Army National Guard. He is a well known and respected trainer in police and military special operations, terrorism and leadership. He has twice received his department's Medal of Valor, and has served two combat tours in the Global War on Terror (G.W.O.T.), one in Afghanistan and one in Iraq. His combat awards include the Bronze Star w/V device, two Bronze Stars and the Combat Infantryman's Badge. He may be reached at randyw@ci.ogden.ut.us.

GOOD VS. EVIL: A STORY ABOUT WINNING

by Marcus Young

While working a graveyard shift as a patrol sergeant, I was shot multiple times, including a .38 caliber round through the head. My right arm was broken and paralyzed and my left hand was physically ripped apart. Kneeling with my butt resting against my heels in a parking stall of the dimly lit parking lot of Wal-Mart, I looked down and saw my badge thickly covered with my own blood. My pulse was racing, blood pressure elevated, and respiration was too fast. My thoughts were...I need to slow down my rate of breathing otherwise I will lose consciousness. By using a controlled breathing exercise, I lowered my physiological response after being critically injured...moments later I heard the many sirens.

On the night of March 7, I worked an overtime shift as a patrol sergeant for the Ukiah Police Department. Riding along with me was a 17-year-old high school student and uniformed police cadet, Julian Covella. A little before 9:30 PM we responded to a call concerning a female shoplifter at the local Wal-Mart. I parked my marked patrol car in the front lot and Covella and I entered the store. The store manager directed us to the security office in the back of the store where two security guards detained the suspect, 18 year-old Monica Winnie. She had fraudulently returned a duffle bag (valued at $ 29.00) to the store for cash. The security guard told me there was a male accomplice wearing a brown bomber jacket and identifiable by tattoos on his neck waiting outside the store. After taking custody of Winnie, I escorted her to my patrol unit with Covella following. I asked the security guards and assistant manager to locate the accomplice and direct him to me. Winnie told me that her boyfriend had no weapons and I had no reason be to be concerned about my safety. Later, the accomplice was identified as a 35-year-old Neal Beckman.

There is no routine call

After I secured Winnie in the backseat of my patrol car suspect Beckman confronted me in the parking lot. He asked me why his girlfriend was in the car. I intended to evaluate him for drug influence and interview him about his role in the theft. His hands were shoved in his jacket pockets when I asked him to remove them. He said that he had a knife and began to move his left hand from his jacket pocket. Winnie began screaming and I cleared the distance between Beckman and myself taking control of Beckman's left arm and putting it in a control hold which positioned me shoulder to shoulder with him. At the same time Beckman managed to remove a .38 caliber, five shot revolver, with his right hand from his right jacket pocket. He reached across his chest and over his left shoulder and fired the first round through my head. The bullet went through my left cheek and exited the back of my neck millimeters away from my spine. We struggled onto a vehicle and then to the ground. While Beckman continued to fire his gun all five rounds struck me. My soft body armor ultimately stopped two potentially fatal rounds. I took two shots to my left front and rear torso and another round struck me in my mid-back with the bullet fracturing my scapula, nearly missing my spine.

The fifth shot to my right bicep shattered the humerus bone, destroying muscle tissue, and caused paralysis to my entire right arm. My left hand was physically ripped apart roughly two inches between the left middle and index finger during my ensuing life and death struggle. The security guard intervened to save my life, but Beckman brutally stabbed him in the left side of his chest and shoulder area. Beckman then ran to my patrol unit entering the right front passenger door. He did not intend to release his girlfriend, but to retrieve the fully automatic weapon or the Remington 870 shotgun from my marked patrol unit.

Fighting to win

I was now kneeling with my butt resting against my heels in the dimly lit Wal-Mart parking lot about a stall and a half away from my patrol car. I looked down and saw my badge thickly covered with my own blood. My chest, shoulders, and arms were also covered with blood. I knew I had been shot multiple times including one in the face. My right arm was paralyzed and my left hand had been ripped apart. I thought: "I'm bleeding to death, but I have to stop the suspect." I saw people running in the parking lot and public safety remained a concern. Besides my own safety, I was concerned for the safety of the teenage cadet who had taken cover nearby and the security guard who lay in the parking lot bleeding to death. I thought that if I didn't stop the suspect he would kill us or anyone else in the parking lot. I wasn't able to draw my .40 caliber from my holster with either hand because of my injuries. I called for Covella to come to my side asking him to remove my weapon and place it in my injured left hand. Aiming at Beckman and the patrol car I fired my perfectly functioning gun four times before stopping him. Beckman was pronounced dead on arrival at the hospital. At this point, I felt close to losing consciousness and I needed to slow down my breathing and lower my blood pressure otherwise I would bleed out and die. I directed Covella to radio dispatch notifying "Officer Down" and to use my flashlight to summon emergency personnel when they arrived on scene. Using a controlled breathing exercise I slowed down my heart rate and blood pressure. Moments later I heard the many sirens.

A Spouse's Perspective

My wife Stephanie best describes what happened in the hours and days to follow:

> *"Friends stayed with our son and daughter while I waited to hear from the doctor at the hospital. Two officers from our police association came to talk to me. We discussed facts about the incident, the investigation, the attorney interviews that Marcus would have to give, items booked as evidence, and the bad guys family. I didn't realize thoughts of retaliation where already looming. It was overwhelming and yet this was just the beginning. My sister and I stood by Marcus' side while a flood of doctors and nurses poked and prodded him and the puddles of blood around him just kept getting bigger. He hadn't been given medications yet because of the gunshot wound to his head and significant blood loss. I tried to talk to Marcus without being emotional even though it was killing me inside to see him flat on his back and in pain, - well I assumed he was in pain because he was*

shot up, but never complained. Every time I turned my attention away from him lying there I would look up to the foot of the bed to see a sea of law enforcement officers. I had never seen so many different uniforms milling around such a tight area. One officer didn't leave his side and I kept thinking he can go now. Later I found out that when something like this happens an officer is assigned to stay with his injured brother. As Marcus was being prepped for surgery he asked me to go find Julian, the cadet, and I promised I would tell Julian that he was very brave, that Marcus was very proud of him, and that Julian saved Marcus' life. There are hundreds of decisions after your husband is injured and you don't have much time to make them without even realizing that you are being pulled between hospital staff, law enforcement visitors, family, friends, and your own duty to your family. I needed to protect my kids and my husband not only physically, but emotionally as well, as the investigation still loomed overhead."

The Aftermath

Neil Beckman was an affiliated gang member who had spent significant time in prison. At the time of the incident, he was wanted for felony charges associated with a home invasion robbery. That night, Beckman was armed with a stolen and fully load .38 caliber five shot revolver, a hunting knife, and five explosive devices. Because the security guard and Covella had courageously risked their lives for my own, I am alive today. They both received numerous awards including the Carnegie Hills Medal, a Mayor's Medal of Valor, and the California Narcotics

Officers Association Citizens of the Year Award. Since the incident Covella was hired as a police officer for the Ukiah Police Department and currently works as a solo patrol officer.

Over the past five years, I have presented my experience to numerous audiences throughout the United States focusing on the following lessons learned:

Mental Preparedness

Mentally prepare yourself before beginning your shift with the goal of returning home regardless of the circumstances. Although I was shot five times, I continued to fight until I stopped the suspect, never give up the fight.

Value the Ride-a-long

Communicate with your ride-a-long about theoretical possibilities because he or she may be forced into a situation to save your life. Although the 17-year-old cadet had not trained to remove a handgun from a holster, his brave actions were imperative to our survival. Because no other units were available that night I had neglected to call for assistance before confronting the second suspect (Beckman). Knowing there was a second suspect involved, described as a parolee type, I could have called an allied agency for assistance. The security guard and police cadet came to my assistance. Never under estimate the value of courageous people around you.

Tactics

Because of my close proximity to the suspect I instinctively closed the distance to control the suspect's movements. If my distance were greater I could have moved to a position of cover and removed my firearm, ordering the suspect to turn around and slowly remove each hand from his pockets while directing him into a felony prone position, calling for backup. Rehearse the same scenario with the suspect having a handgun and knife in each pocket. Regardless of the circumstances, I would have been at a greater advantage by having the suspect turn around before asking him to remove his hands from his jacket pockets.

Ongoing Training

Regularly train to exceed the minimum departmental and state requirements for use of force knowledge and skills (i.e. weaponless defense, chemical agents, electronic devices, impact weapons, and firearms). Without this on-going developmental proficiency skills practice fundamental skills will likely diminish over time. In high stress situations you will likely utilize those techniques which have been practiced countless times and are most familiar to you.

An Officer Involved Shooting

Familiarize yourself with all aspects of an officer involved shooting (OIS) investigation which will include evidence collection. During my incident an investigation was conducted by the Department of Justice, District Attorney's Office, my agency, and the insurance company.

Multiple agencies were involved in the initial response and following investigation. Unless there are exigent circumstances in the interest of public safety have legal representation before beginning the interview process. Upon arrival at the hospital I requested the emergency room nurse to take two blood samples for drug and alcohol screening. All of my duty gear and clothing were seized as evidence with the exception of my briefs. Prepare and educate your family members in what to expect in the event of an OIS or off-duty confrontation, including expectations for family members if confronted off-duty.

Debriefing

The debriefing process should involve all those involved during the critical incident (e.g. police officers, emergency responders, dispatchers, supervisors, administrators, and family members). Take the time necessary to heal physically and mentally. Our mission to survive law enforcement should go beyond our career and retirement years. It is imperative that we tactically debrief critical incidents to learn from these experiences to benefit others in law enforcement.

Overcoming Obstacles

My faith in God gave me the strength to overcome adversity during and after the incident, including overcoming subsequent surgeries and rehabilitation. I am forever grateful for the ongoing support of family, friends, community members, and our greater law enforcement community. During my career many inspirational trainers (i.e. defensive tactic instructors, range masters, and martial artists) challenged me physically, mentally, and spiritually. These people were instrumental to my continued successes in overcoming adversity throughout my career. Great trainers taught me the importance of lifelong learning, staying calm under pressure, resourcefulness, and how to fight regardless of the circumstances.

Quite simply, I was trained to fight through pain and never give up.

Marcus Young is a twenty-year veteran of law enforcement. He graduated from the University of San Francisco with a Master's degree in Counseling Psychology and Bachelor's degree in Organizational Behavior. Marcus serves his community and Mendocino College as the Director of Public Safety Programs. President George W. Bush and Governor Arnold Schwarzenegger awarded Marcus with a Medal of Valor. The International Association of Chiefs of Police recognized Marcus as the Officer of the Year. Marcus has presented to audiences throughout the United States. You can contact Marcus at xyoung@comcast.net.

TACTICAL MINDSET

by Massad Ayoob

"The mind is the weapon. All else is supplemental." The great novelist John Steinbeck wrote those words. Lt. Col. Jeff Cooper, USMC (ret.), a great trainer of warriors, popularized them. Those two thoughts are so strongly and widely remembered because they are true.

This book is dedicated to people who go in harm's way. They will wear different uniforms. They will work in units of varying strength, to accomplish a wide variety of necessary missions. They will have to comply with certain rules of engagement. Though each will probably have been told at some time in their training, "Keep It Simple," they will face infinitely complicated problems they will be expected to solve almost instantaneously.

Those who read this publication will have been trained in the use of various force options. They will have been taught to fight with their hands and feet and other "body weapons" if they have nothing else to fight with. Some, particularly in the law enforcement and professional security sectors, will rely heavily on "less-lethal" force tools. Most, at least when in action, will be equipped with lethal weapons that will vary as to range and firepower depending on the mission. Some will even be charged with controlling weapons of mass destruction in time of war.

Whatever the level of force at their disposal, no matter how rigid the command structure or the Rules of

Engagement, the time will come when each of them has to make an independent decision to take a physical action that may result in the predictable death of human beings, sometimes many human beings. And when that act is done, however fair or unfair it may be, they will be judged for it.

When the time comes, those tactical operators will make up their mind to apply force, or will reflexively carry out an action they made up their mind beforehand to respond with automatically when a certain stimulus arose to trigger that particular response. When it is over, they will have to explain what was in their mind when they carried out the action that launched that irrevocable destructive force.

Steinbeck was right. Cooper was right.

It will always come back to the mind…

Voices to Listen To

A wise instructor studies and shares the knowledge and collective experience of "the best and the brightest" in the world of contemporary tactics. Our job as trainers is to bring what those people know to the student, the individual who will be putting those tactics to use at a time when human lives are on the line and that student may be the only entity standing between an acceptable resolution of violent conflict, and a most undesirable one. That student's decisions and actions will determine what our colleagues in medicine speak of euphemistically as "good outcomes" and "bad outcomes." What the clergymen and philosophers call simply "good" and "evil."

Non soleus. In Latin, those words mean "never alone." They were made famous among warriors by Col. Robert Lindsey, retired from law enforcement but still active in training. He reminds us that even if we seem to be utterly alone in a life-threatening crisis, we have with us all of those who trained us, all of those who inspired us to fight, and all of those who are counting on us to win the encounter in which we are now embroiled.

"Off duty, but not off watch." Police chief and tactical expert Jeff Chudwin recently coined this phrase, and it is destined to become a standard concept. Soldiers remember the kidnapping of General Dozier from his home by terrorists. Any police officer can tell you of a colleague who was caught off guard when off duty. There is no situation a warrior will face that will be more demanding of the element of mindset.

"Be prepared for the fight itself, *and* be prepared for the aftermath." We work in a world where our actions are constantly judged, often by those who have little if any ethical right to judge them. The soldier who puts a final, anchoring bullet through the brain of a suicidal terrorist bomber knows that these days, he may face court martial. The police officer who sees a suspect's hand lunging as if for a weapon knows as he reaches for his own gun that if his assessment of the danger is incorrect, powerful voices will call for him to be sent to prison. Yet in each situation, hesitation can mean death for the operator, and/or death to those innocents he has sworn an oath to protect. If he does not know that he can confidently face the aftermath, he may hesitate in a moment when there is no time for hesitation, and his life and the lives of those innocents may come to an abrupt end. The student must learn to develop confidence in managing the aftermath that equals his or her confidence in your ability to win the fight itself.

You will hear from doctors who will give you insight into how your mind and your body work when engaged in mortal combat. You will hear voices from the cutting edge of proven, modern training that can help prepare you for that moment. Herbert Spencer said, "Policemen are soldiers who act alone, soldiers are policemen who act in unison." Yet cop and soldier alike may have to fight alone in a dark alley, whether that alley is in Chicago or Baghdad. Soldier and cop may stand shoulder to shoulder with brothers and sisters, military squad or SWAT team alike, but will still have to individually decide whether to pull that trigger.

The wise instructor will bring all these voices to the ears of the student. The wise student will listen.

The training, the preparation, and the decision itself at the unforgiving moment when it must be implemented, go far beyond the tools. It's not just about the gun and the knife, the club and the fist. It's about the mind that controls all of those weapons.

>Steinbeck was right. Cooper was right.

"The mind is the weapon. All else is supplemental."

Capt. Massad Ayoob has served some three and a half decades as a fully sworn law enforcement officer, working that job part time, and nearly as long as a full-time trainer in the use of force. He is the founder and director of Lethal Force Institute, has been widely published in police, firearms, and martial arts magazines, and is the author of several books and training tapes on the judicious use of deadly force. He has appeared in many courts as an expert witness speaking on behalf of police officers and armed citizens who have had to kill in self-defense. The winner of the 1998 Outstanding American Handgunner of the Year award, Ayoob has taught for IALEFI, served approximately 20 years as chair of the firearms committee of ASLET, and has been a member of the advisory board of ILEETA since its inception.

CULTIVATING THE WARRIOR SPIRIT
by Sgt. Gregg W. Gaby

Why on earth would you want to be a Police Officer? All of us have heard this or something similar from someone during our careers. Some of us may have even asked ourselves this question. Why are we drawn to a profession that is constantly being second guessed by politicians, the media, expert witnesses and attorneys whose only interest are normally self serving? After years of listening to applicants for my department, we all seem to have chosen law enforcement for the same basic reasons; to help others or to protect and serve. We are doers of good and fighters of evil. I believe that most everyone entering this profession truly wants to do well for their fellow man, but is everyone in our profession prepared and qualified for the demands of modern policing? What makes that hard charging recruit become cynical and disillusioned with the job? I think anyone would be kidding him or her self if he or she thinks this could be answered with one simple statement. As a tactical officer and trainer, I believe that with proper planning most obstacles can be prevented or overcome before they are encountered. I believe this is also true in training or preparing a recruit or new member of a department for their new career. I have been to countless use of force classes that have prepared me for the technical application of force, but very few have tapped into the spirit of why we must do our job when the time comes.

As a trainer you are a leader. You decide whether you are good or bad, but make no mistake, you are a leader. As a leader you have a role and responsibility to cultivate the spirit of a warrior in each person you are assigned to train. This does not mean only the technical or mechanical side of the job, but to instill in them the values and tradition of a noble and honorable profession. To show them that law enforcement officers are about preserving life, even if it means having to take a life. To get them to understand that our tradition includes many honorable men and women who died defending the common threads that bind us all together in Law Enforcement.

What makes an officer return to the job after facing a deadly force encounter and taking a human life? Speaking from personal experience, I can honestly say that it was not the technical knowledge that I had received over the years. Make no mistake, all of my training has been invaluable and guided me throughout my law enforcement career. I am by no means downplaying the importance of sharpening our technical skills on the range or in the gym. The point I am trying to make is that as trainers we must possess and teach a belief system. A person practicing the art of war without a just cause or righteous belief in winning is a war monger, not a warrior. There are many great fighters and athletes practicing various fighting arts on television. While they may be great fighters, they are not warriors. To cultivate the spirit in the warrior, we must ensure that all officers believe in the nobility of the profession they have chosen. They must understand that they are not one, but part of a great culture that stands between good and evil in our society. They need to be proud of what they do and how they do it. As Lt. Col Dave Grossman puts it, we are the Sheepdogs protecting the sheep from the wolves. So who is training and caring for the Sheepdogs in your agency?

I recently had the privilege of training another recruit class for my agency. One day, before their normal lunch break, I gave them a map to a cemetery and had them meet me at a grave side. The grave marked the final resting place of a hero - a third generation police officer from our department who died in the line of duty. His name is Jason "Jake" Grossnickle. At the grave side, we met Officer Rob Cleaver, who graduated the academy with Jason and had been with him – a mere four months after this graduation - during a fight for their lives. After being ambushed, Rob was nearly killed and watched his classmate die. He spoke to the recruit class and gave them the horrible details of what happened on the day Jason died and he was shot in the face and left for dead. Rob fought back and survived that day. He is a warrior and a true hero. He has a profound personal and professional belief system and is still a productive member and K-9 handler within our department. It would have been real easy for him to never return to work after experiencing something as tragic as this, especially so early in his career, but he did return. After listening to Rob's experiences, I asked each recruit to place their hand on Jason's headstone and promise themselves that they would never do anything to disgrace the honor of Jason, his father, and hisgGrandfather, as well as everyone who has died while wearing the badge and uniform of our department. This was not a religious oath, but a promise to honor the sacrifice of those who have helped pave the way in our profession.

I am sure that all of you have heroes from your agencies. These are the people that need to be recognized when teaching the path to the young warrior. There are many dramatic and even subtle ways to cultivate the spirit of the warrior in your department. Something as simple as creating a challenge coin for the officers on your squad or department can be a simple step on the path to instilling tradition and pride. All officers must be taught their roles as warriors, from the first day of basic training or the day that they raise their hand and take the oath as officers on the department. Have them examine every word of the oath that they swore to uphold on the first day of their appointment. Make them realize that they are promising to carry on the traditions and responsibility of each and every law enforcement officer who has served before them.

There is no room for cynicism or hypocrisy when training the new warrior. How can we expect the newest recruit to believe in a system that we portray as negative. I have to admit that this has been the biggest personal challenge for me as a trainer and a supervisor. There are or will be bad times in all of our lives and careers. It is how we handle these situations that will define us in the eyes of the people we are tasked to train. We must personally hold tight to the principles and beliefs that we are trying to instill, or face certain failure as a trainer and a leader. The laissez faire approach to training a warrior is even more ineffective than it is in day to day leadership.

How do we keep our motivation as trainers? I personally have a great network of fellow trainers and many have authored chapters in this book. As our department's training supervisor, I was recently tasked to provide leadership training for every supervisor within our Department. I was fortunate enough to have attended a session with Bill Westfall at the 2006 ILEETA conference. I arranged to have Mr. Westfall conduct the leadership training for our department. As he taught the differences between the manager and a leader, he pointed out that leaders do the right thing and managers do things right. And so, I ask you to seek out the fellow trainers who are doing the right thing, not just doing things right!

If you are reading this, I hope you have an interest in making one of the noblest professions in the world better. I love being part of a profession that allows me to walk with giants on a daily basis. Some of the truest heroes and greatest warriors I have ever met are the men and women in blue, which brings me to my final points.

- Do you walk the walk and not just talk the talk?
- Do you believe that law enforcement is one of the most noble and honorable professions ever?
- Do you use words such as courage, integrity and loyalty and live by them?

If you can honestly answer yes to these questions then you are obligated to pass on your knowledge to the next generation of warriors that have chosen our profession. It is your job to cultivate the warrior spirit within them and our profession.

Sergeant Gaby is a 21 year veteran of the Dayton (OH) Police Department. His current duty assignment is the Training Supervisor for the Dayton Police Academy where he is responsible for recruit and in-service training for the department. His past assignments have included Patrol Operations, Bike Squad, FTO, Operations Supervisor, full time range officer and instructor. He has served as a member of the Dayton SWAT Team for 19 years and his duties on the tactical team have included Operator, Precision Rifleman, Team Leader and Acting Commander. He is also an instructor for the National Tactical Officers Association and veteran of the United States Marine Corps.

STAY DANGEROUS

by George Demetriou

There are no dangerous weapons;
There are only dangerous men.
We're trying to teach you to be dangerous
to the enemy.
Dangerous even without a knife.
Deadly as long as you still have one hand or one
foot and are still alive.

— Robert Heinlein

In a profession where one never knows if the person being made contact with has the desire, will and ability to kill you there is only one good option...to be dangerous.

The alternative to being professionally dangerous is to hope that nothing bad happens. If you're reading this you already know that "hope" is not a strategy.

You are professionally dangerous when physically, mentally, spiritually and emotionally prepared to respond efficiently to violence against you or those you serve. It is the ability to "flick the internal switch" that allows you to go from mere presence to using whatever level of force is appropriate without a long analytical pause. It is being physically fit enough to fight for your life with a determined attacker. It is training of the mind and body, together with the tools you carry, and having effective responses for the attacks which have brought many before you to the hospital or morgue. These include close up and sudden assaults with empty hands, edged weapons and firearms. It is the ability to use the training you have in a wide variety of circumstances including the ones you didn't think of previously and were not specifically trained for. It is being adaptive.

By studying the dynamics of violent offender confrontations we observe common tactics used by the attackers and learn what makes an officer successfully defend against them or fall victim to them.

Being dangerous also means understanding that the vast majority of officers seriously injured or killed by violent offenders are done so at very close range. Professionally dangerous officers realize that there is safety in keeping distance, but that it is not always possible. Professionally dangerous officers realize that sudden attacks are the deadliest. The law enforcer will often not have time on his or her side.

Physical Conditioning

"Combat offers randomized challenges that are largely anaerobic, completely functional, and mixed generously between the lower extremities, trunk/core and upper extremities. Any program that doesn't readily match and train for these demands is woefully lacking."
    -Greg Glassman, founder of CrossFit,
    March 2003, CrossFit Journal

"Understand that mental toughness is born of adversity. That it will atrophy if not consistently engaged; and that it carries over to everything you do."
    -Jason Dougherty, U.S. Marine and CrossFitter,
    May 2008 CrossFit Journal

Violent confrontations will place a high demand on the body. Heart rates will rise sharply and muscles will be taxed through both physical exertion and combat stress. Physical conditioning that supports the ability to handle intense exertion and the fear response during a life and death confrontation must be intense and varied. Workouts without intensity do little to prepare officers for the type of fitness that is part of everyday police work. Body building and long, slow runs have nothing to do with the dynamics of an actual critical incident that law enforcers are involved in. Law enforcers sprint, jump, squat, lift, pull their body weight or someone else, push, climb and fight. These are movements that require the whole body functioning as one unit. The movements in the workouts should replicate this in form and intensity.

There exists the curse of believing one is in "good shape." A person who trains at all is in good shape compared to the person who does nothing. However, this is not the standard that is acceptable for winning a life and death fight. The officer with the body builder or marathon runner regime may believe he is in "good shape," but we have to ask, in good shape for what? Being extremely lean or well muscled does not mean being functional for a winning performance when a determined violent offender attempts to impose his will.

Workouts should include power movements, explosiveness, speed, and cardio-respiratory work that are short in duration, but intense. The workouts should reflect the work output that an officer experiences when he chases a suspect at a sprint and then has to fight with him. The workouts should reflect the work output an officer experiences when locked in close combat with a larger and stronger assailant. If an officer cannot sprint 100 meters and still have enough in the gas tank to fight a determined, larger attacker he is NOT in "good shape."

In order to be dangerous law enforcers need the kind of toughness that enables them to win the life and death fight when they are wounded, out-gunned, out numbered or when faced with a highly motivated violent offender. There are few options available for on-going mental toughness training, but intense physical training makes the trainee mentally tough. If the workouts are conducted correctly there will come a point when the officer will want to stop because the fatigue factor is greatly elevated. The officer will have to leave his "comfort zone." Pushing past that zone of comfort will toughen the officer mentally. The same drive that causes one to continue the workout will translate to staying in the fight during a violent event. The mere act of committing to regular intense workouts facilitates mental toughness. Training to keep going, no matter what, removes the desire to quit when fatigued or injured.

Recognizing the Pre-Attack Indicators

Recognizing those behavioral indicators which usually precede an assault is crucial for buying time. The Pre-Attack Indicators are:

The perp scan: Side to side movement of the head, eyes scanning as far as they can in both directions. This indicates that the suspect is looking to see if there are any witnesses and/or what the best escape route is.

Drastic facial expression change: As calm as an offender may try to be once he or she begins to mentally process an escape or attack his or her face will, in many cases, reflect tension. Some will have a facial twitch while others get a look of dread.

The subtle forward weight shift: The offender is getting ready to "launch" his body forward quickly and aggressively.

Shoulder forward, chin drop, knee flex: All these movements protect vital spots on the body in anticipation of a clash or attack.

Behavior that doesn't "fit" in the context of the contact: Removing a hat when leaving a car, suddenly dropping into a squat while speaking to the officer, talking and turning away, the subtle look at the officer's firearm.

Feeling/touching motions near the waistband or pocket: Subconscious "checking" to make sure their weapon is there and the hand is close by for quick access.

Conversation that doesn't "fit" in the context of the contact: When South Carolina Trooper Mark Coates was killed in the early 90s the entire vehicle stop, field interview, assault and murder was captured by dash board camera. During the interview Trooper Coates asks the driver if he has "any weapons, guns, knives or hand grenades." The driver's response was, *"Well...."* And his voice trails off. *"Well,"* as an answer to that question is a bad sign. Anything other than "No" as an answer means it's time to take a different course of action. Moments later the driver pulled a small handgun from his pocket, assaulted Trooper Coates, and killed him.

Phrases such as, *"I can't go back to jail,"* or *"We're going to have a problem"* as well as phrases that make absolutely no sense at all are indications that something is wrong and it's time to back out, get back up or in the very least acknowledge to yourself that something bad may be about to happen and you should have a response ready.

Skill Set of the Dangerous Professional

"You better have some personal capacity for dealing with threatening circumstances."

- John S. Farnam

We live in the information age. We can see real assaults on people and police officers included on video, television, or the internet. Assault details are recorded and statistics kept. There are no secrets when it comes to how violent offenders attack civilians or police officers. Most law enforcers killed are killed by offenders with handguns. Cops are assaulted by weapons of the body---punches, elbows, head butts. They are grabbed and struck. They are pulled to the ground. They are tackled. Law enforcers are attacked by offenders with edged weapons, baseball bats and other objects.

The focus, for the law enforcer should be on how the violent offender sets up and pulls off their attacks. Offenders take advantage of what they perceive as weakness and inattentiveness on the part of officers and make use of surprise, cunning and distraction.

For the unprepared officer, the surprise and time advantage taken by the offender will often lead the offender into another advantage--violence of action. While the officer is attempting to respond, get some kind of control—stop or at least slow the violence against him, the offender continues the onslaught, imposing his will, causing damage and dictating how the event will play out. The unprepared officer is "stuck" trying to "catch-up" with his own reactions, attempting to minimize the damage, attempting to remember something effective to do in this particular type of incident and all the while being concerned with department policy.

The dangerous law enforcers know what the common unarmed attacks are and they have a response for them. There should be as few responses as possible for a wide variety of attacks. When the subconscious mind is searching for a response to sudden violence you want to make sure it isn't bogged down with multiple choices to sort through, the fewer responses the better. Stopping the initial attack prevents the incident from evolving into a deadly threat incident as unarmed attacks could lead to the officer being dragged to the ground, stomped and disarmed

Armed assaults mostly consist of handguns and edged weapons. The danger is in approaching a suspect and having the suspect suddenly produce a weapon. Dangerous officers understand and train to keep a safe distance when it is feasible, but they also understand that they must sharpen their skill set for very close proximity. The dangerous officer knows he must treat all sudden, aggressive arm motion as if the offender had a weapon in his hands. Not to do so is to hesitate and remain in reaction mode too long.

The Skill Set Must Also Include:

Weapon retention: It must be remembered that attempting to retain a firearm is still a fight and you must act accordingly. There have been occasions when officers were attempting a retention "technique" when they could have just as easily used impact force to keep the would-be gun grabber away.

Ground fighting and ground grappling/control: Ground fighting is when the officer is on the ground and the offender is standing over him. In this scenario the offender will usually try to kick or stomp the officer's head or face. Ground grappling/control is when the offender is on the ground with the officer. The offender will usually try to "mount" the officer and punch or disarm the officer.

Moving and shooting while approaching a stopped vehicle: Incidents of offenders shooting officers while performing traffic stops has increased. Officers must train to move on the best angles to offer protection or in the very least make it difficult for the offender to shoot them.

Moving and shooting while a gunman approaches a stopped police vehicle: There have been cases of offenders rushing police vehicles to shoot the cops in their cars. Officers need to train for moving the vehicle out quickly or moving themselves out of the vehicle while engaging the offender.

Combating the cuff pull: Offenders who have co-operated to the point of being cuffed on one arm and then suddenly pulling that arm away before the officer can get the second handcuff on. This gives the offender the opportunity to fight or draw a concealed weapon while the officer "chases" the handcuffed arm. Officers need to disregard trying to recapture the cuffed arm and go right to control of the offender or engaging with the firearm.

The Mentality of the Professionally Dangerous

An officer approaches a man he needs to investigate for whatever reason. The officer can see the suspect has nothing in his hands. There is a brief conversation. Suddenly the suspect has a gun, a knife or some object in his hand and he is moving it toward the officer's direction. What happened between there being nothing in the suspect's hand and the suspect having a weapon in his hand? There may have been a momentary lapse of attention or a distraction. Whatever the case, the professionally dangerous officer is aware at all times.

Being and staying dangerous is first and foremost a mentality that all law enforcers should possess. Officers are killed when they become complacent and when they fail to "see the signs." All officers know, at some level, that there are predatory humans, but many believe they won't encounter them. The officers who are dangerous figure they will come across the worst violent offender one day so they prepare every day.

Being and staying dangerous requires that officers stay sharp with their personal weapons, tools they carry and their firearms. Fighting is fighting whether it's with bare hands, intermediate weapons or firearms. Dangerous officers understand that in order to be victorious they must be fighters.

The mentality of the professionally dangerous dictates that should an offender attempt to use violence the officer involved will go into action with a clear mind, no hesitation, no dithering and do whatever it takes to overcome any assault.

The professionally dangerous officers use controlled aggression. They decide to be aggressive enough quickly enough.

The professionally dangerous law enforcers possess defiance. They don't accept that they should be victims or that their fate should be determined by a violent criminal.

> *"This is the law:*
> *The purpose of fighting is to win;*
> *There is no possible victory in defense,*
> *The sword is more important than the shield,*
> *And skill is more important than either.*
> *The final weapon is the brain.*
> *All else is supplemental."*
>
> - John Steinbeck

George Demetriou is a retired New York Police Department Detective. George's duties included uniformed patrol, mobile response task force, community patrol, plainclothes anti-crime, narcotics enforcement, organized crime investigation and international terrorism investigation.

George has been on the staff of Modern Warrior Defensive Tactics Institute for nearly 20 years.

George is the owner/Director of Spartan Performance. Spartan Performance is dedicated to functional fitness, using the CrossFit methodology, and performance during the dynamics of violent offender confrontations.

George has been published in Law and Order, American Police Beat, The Trainer, Police Marksman, and the Illinois Tactical Officers Association magazine and the ILEETA Journal.

George has presented or co-presented for the American Society of Law Enforcement Trainers (ASLET), International Law Enforcement Educators and Trainers Association (ILEETA), Western Canada Use of Force, TREXPO and the American Woman's Self defense Association (AWSDA) conferences.

Training to Win

"...the Warrior who has trained anad practiced, pushing his muscles and his mind to the limit over and over again, preparing for just this moment in time, this Warrior has never been so alive. Of all the places in the world, at this exact moment in time, he is precsisely where he belongs - facing evil in battle. His mind is crystal clear and firing on all cylinders. Every one of his senses are finely tuned as though he has radar vision in a 360 degree radius. He is striking, slamming, drawing, moving and yelling commands. He does not stop until he has WON. He is a Warrior in battle, and at that moment his sole purpose for existing is to close with evil and crush it."

- Gary Stoney

TRAINING TO WIN

by Brian Willis

For many years in law enforcement training we have talked about the Survival State of Mind, Officer Survival and the Survival Mindset. This philosophy was on the leading edge of mental preparation and conditioning training 25 years ago and has played a critical role in the advancement of officer safety training. The time has come however, to advance this philosophy to the next level in the continual evolution of law enforcement training. This requires a fundamental shift from training officers to Survive to training them to WIN. Every year in North America hundreds of officers are victims of violent assaults in which they survive, but as a result are seriously injured, and in some cases permanently disabled. We have to respect and admire these officers for surviving these violent encounters; however, we are left to wonder what the outcome may have been if they had been trained to win and not just survive; if they had been trained to be the predator and not the prey. The best way to honor these officers is to learn from their experiences. The first step in the transition to 'Training to Win' is to accept the reality that for many officers 'Survival' is completely defensive in nature. Accepting this reality allows us to train to reprogram this response.

Unfortunately some people still mistakenly believe that the philosophy of training officers to win is tantamount to training them to be paranoid, to over react, to respond emotionally by using excessive force and brutalizing subjects. Nothing could be further from the truth. Winning takes many forms and ranges from an officer's professional presence and use of effective communication skills to gain voluntary compliance from a subject, to killing the subject to protect the life of the officer or someone else. Training to win is about developing the competence and confidence that allows officers to be calm, focused, in-control and confident in any situation. It is about developing the ability to assess situations and respond in a manner that is both reasonable and necessary based upon the totality of the circumstances. It is also about having the verbal and non-verbal communication skills to be able to interact with victims, witnesses and subjects in a clear, concise and professional manner. It is about being a professional who embodies the Core Values of the organization.

Training to win requires officers to accept some fundamental truths about life as law enforcement professionals. Officers who train to win understand the realities and the science of action versus reaction, and time and distance. Training to win requires an understanding of when disengaging to create distance, time and options is most appropriate and when closing on the subject taking away their time and options is most desirable. It is about accepting and understanding the difference between killing and murder. Murder is the taking of an innocent life while killing to protect self and others is authorized by law and supported by society. Training to win requires officers to accept that as law enforcement professionals they may have to take a life, to kill another human being, in order to save a life. It also involves an understanding that the only acceptable option in any confrontation is winning. Tying or losing are acceptable options in sporting events, not in violent encounters.

Control

Control is an important element of training to win. An officer who is in control of himself or herself resulting from a high degree of competence and confidence in their skills, tactics and knowledge will more easily be able to control subjects and situations. Competent, confident professional officers use their professional presence as well as their conflict resolution and crisis intervention skills effectively to consistently win on the street and in court.

Commitment

Commitment is another important element in training to win. This requires every officer to make a personal commitment to train on their own throughout his or her career to enhance skills, tactics, fitness and mental preparation. Those not committed to winning make excuses why they can't train and abdicate the responsibility for training to their agency. They have the mentality that training should always be: "on the company time, and on the company dime." They refuse to invest their own time and money on training. They will often invest in stocks, bonds and real estate, but refuse to invest in training that could save their life or the life of someone else. They rationalize their lack of commitment to training by saying "If the training was that important the department would provide it or pay for me to go." This is a dangerous mindset. This is a victim mentality. This mindset gets people killed. These officers fail to comprehend the reality that there never has been, and there never will be, a law enforcement agency killed or injured in the line of duty. Agencies do not respond to calls, make traffic stops, search buildings or make arrests. Law enforcement officers however perform those tasks every day. It is the rank and file officers that respond to calls for service, not agencies. Officers, not agencies, get killed and injured in the line of duty. Therefore officers must take responsibility for their life and make a personal commitment to continually train their mind and body by continually seeking out opportunities to train on their own.

Offense and Not Defense

Winning is about offense. In order to win officers need to condition themselves to act and think offensively rather than defensively. If a team only plays defense in a sporting event the best they can hope for is a tie. A tie still earns them a point in the league standings. On the street there are no ties, and a loss for the law enforcement officer can have tragic consequences. In sports the term 'sudden death' creates tension and excitement for the viewing public; for law enforcement officers it can mean adding another name to the memorial walls. Officers who train to win treat every block as an offensive technique designed to attack and destroy the assailant's delivery system. 'Training to win' means accepting that every situation is winnable. This is not the 'Superman Syndrome' where an officer thinks they are impervious to harm because they wear a uniform and carry a badge. Rather it is a powerful acceptance that if they find themselves in a violent encounter, they can and will win it.

Predator and Not Prey

Training to win involves an understanding of the Predator – Prey mentality and an acceptance that winning requires that the officer be the predator and not the prey. For many people the word 'Predator' conjures up very negative images. They tend to think of sexual predators, or the seedy element of society who prey on the weak and the elderly. As a result, it is difficult for some law enforcement officers to understand the important role that the 'Predator Mentality' plays in developing a pattern of training to win. To assist in developing an understanding of the positive aspects of the predator mentality let us look to the animal kingdom. When asked to list the positive traits of predatory animals, those traits and characteristics that allow them to be successful, officers list such qualities as:

- Physical quickness, speed, strength and power
- Mental calmness, focus, control and confidence
- Controlled aggression
- Environmental awareness including the use of concealment, cover and movement
- Understanding one's opponent
- Commitment to the goal/mission

Without these traits predatory animals do not survive. In society we often use images of predatory animals as symbols of strength, power, ferocity and unity because of these traits and characteristics. By taking a step back and examining the list it becomes apparent that these are the same qualities that trainers and organizations work to instill in law enforcement officers during officer safety, firearms and subject control tactics training. The same traits that make the difference between success and failure, life and death in the animal world can also make the difference between being the victor and the victim for law enforcement professionals involved in violent altercations. Lt. Colonel Dave Grossman uses the analogy of Sheep, Wolves and Sheepdogs to make this same point. Col. Grossman also says however that only a predator can hunt a predator. The difference is that we are predators under the authority of law.

Obstacles

Law enforcement officers and trainers may have numerous obstacles to overcome in order to ingrain this attitude. Some officers coming into the profession of law enforcement have never been in a real fight and have little or no exposure to interpersonal human aggression. As a result, they have no idea what it is like to be punched or kicked, to have someone threaten them or to have another human being attempt to hurt or kill them. Some have been taught since they were young children that it is wrong to fight, others are taught to always play fair and many are told at home and at church that violence is never the answer and that it is wrong to kill. All law enforcement professionals must accept that during their career they will be exposed to individuals raised in a culture of violence where they were taught that you must fight to get what you want and protect what is yours. Training to win involves accepting the reality that there are people on the street and in the prisons who are prepared to hurt or kill an officer to keep from going back to jail, as payback for a perceived disrespect or to improve their status within the gang culture.

Our Challenge

The challenge to individual officers is what to do throughout your career to not only maintain those skills and tactics learned at the academy, but to enhance them. If you are one of the 'old dogs' who went through training years ago you need to ask yourself what have you done to upgrade and enhance your skills, tactics and mindset? Old dogs can learn new tricks. More importantly we can learn new skills and tactics and new ways of thinking.

Embracing the shift in philosophies from Survival to Winning will yield positive results for officers and agencies. It will ensure that as law enforcement professionals, officers are always ready to calmly and competently handle the challenges facing law enforcement professionals in 2009 and beyond.

Brian Willis is an internationally recognized trainer and speaker. Brian draws on his 25 years of law enforcement experience as a member of the Calgary Police Service and over 19 years of training experience to provide cutting edge training to law enforcement officers and trainers throughout North America. Brian has been honored with a Lifetime Achievement Award in recognition of his contributions to officer safety training in Canada.

Brian operates Winning Mind Training and Warrior Spirit Books (www.warriorspiritbooks.com) and is the editor of the highly acclaimed books W.I.N.: Critical Issues in Training and Leading Warriors as well as a contributing writer for the book Warriors: On Living With Courage, Discipline and Honor (www.warriorspiritbooks.com).

Brian serves as an Advisory Board member for the International Law Enforcement Educators and Trainers Association (ILEETA), and served as a member of the National Advisory Board for Police Marksman Magazine from 2000 to 2007. He is a member of NTOA, ITOA, IALEFI, National Guild of Hypnotists and the Canadian

Association of Professional Speakers. He is the Editor of the ILEETA Review and writes a regular column for the ILEETA Use of Force Journal. Brian can be reached through his website at www.winningmindtraining.com.

TRAINING THE "GUTTERFIGHTER WAY"

by Steven Mosley

As warrior trainers, we must ensure that our students not only possess a "win at any cost" mindset, but also a fighting system that has been pressure tested. You must instill in them the skills that are going to work no matter where they are or what they are doing. I believe that training the "Gutterfighter Way" is your answer, and will explain why.

Gutterfighting - "The Mental Side"

Every day thousands of people train at a martial arts academy. I think this is awesome! The martial arts are great in helping to develop self-discipline, self-confidence, self-esteem and physical fitness. So what exactly is the problem? Let me ask you a question. Take any student of Karate, Kung Fu, Kenpo, Tae Kwon Do or any other form of martial arts and ask them the following: when was the last time you talked about the violence of a physical encounter? When was the last time you thought about the violence of interpersonal human aggression?

Physical confrontations are brutal! I have been in law enforcement for over 24 years and have seen my share of violence. It is not pretty. It is your duty to prepare each student mentally for this. Let's say some of your students have trained for three to four years, three nights per week for at least one hour per session. Wonderful, I applaud them. They have most likely achieved what is equivalent in most martial arts to a Black Belt rank.

Nevertheless, do they really know if the skills that they have paid their blood sweat, tears and earned money for will serve them when they most need them? The student must be trained to recognize and accept the realities of violent confrontation. Please do not fail in giving them this valuable knowledge. They need your experience. The question you must ask yourself is this: have I tested my techniques, my tactics, and my methods in a realistic environment and ensured that they will work? If you do not know if your skills will work, how will your students ever know?

> *"Will this work so that I can use it instinctively in vital combat against an opponent who is determined to prevent me from doing so, and who is striving to eliminate me by fair means or foul?"*
>
> - Lt. Col. Rex Applegate, Kill Or Get Killed

As you may know, when faced with a violent confrontation, most people will run (flight), attack (fight) or freeze. When the mind and body have not been prepared in unison, it has been my observational experience that most people will do nothing when faced with a confrontation. I have even witnessed seasoned law enforcement and military personnel display the "deer in headlights" expression because they had not developed the correct mindset to handle these stressful encounters. They certainly had been trained in the physical skills, but they just had not received the correct mental programming.

One can achieve the will to win through reality-based training. Here are two simple examples of training that will make a world of difference for any practitioner. For one thing, a very high percentage of physical assaults occur in reduced-light situations. It is the perfect environment for the bad guy. When is the last time you turned the lights down in your dojo or training facility and practiced your techniques in reduced light? Secondly, when was the last time you practiced your self-defense skills in the clothes that you wear every day, and not the clothes that you wear to the training facility? I rarely wear sweat pants, nor do I carry on daily activities in a Gi! Practice these two simple training drills, coupled with some true threat assessment and you are well on your way to winning. I am all about winning. Please begin training yourself and your students with reality in mind.

Gutterfighting – "The Physical Side"

I teach a system that borrows its name from the Defendu techniques developed by Fairbairn and Sykes. The name given to our system is "Gutterfighting."

"When you're caught, you're down, and you're a goner if you don't ATTACK…And keep in mind, it's 'Gutterfighting': any means, fair or foul, to save your life."

- W.E. Fairbairn

Our system of Gutterfighting is a blend of Krav Maga, Filipino Martial Arts, World War II Combatives, and Grappling skills. Each of these styles of fighting has certainly been pressure tested in battle. Our Gutterfigthing is all about "fighting" and "winning." One of the most interesting principles of our system of fighting is to rapidly charge at the threat, get as close as possible and finish him off before he can counterattack. Never wait for the attack. Once an imminent danger is observed, attack with all the meanness of a caged animal and don't stop until your opponent is no longer a threat.

I have done my best to ensure that our Gutterfighting has been designed to stand up against the pressures and strain of an all-out confrontation. It is a collection of offenses and defenses in which the smallest person can successfully defeat a larger opponent. It is brutally effective, easy to learn and retain. Gutterfighting is not about fighting pretty. It is all about going beyond just survival and truly winning over your aggressor, which I believe and preach daily! We want our students to win from a legal, mental and physical perspective, and our mission is to teach them to do just that.

Our Gutterfighting training practices combine the use of simple equipment and body weight exercises with focus mitt and Thai pad striking drills in a circuit-training format. This method of this madness is to help better prepare us for the stress of a violent confrontation! We believe in being "Fit to Fight." As previously stated, violent confrontations are brutal; your students must have the stamina to stay in the fight until they have won. The great champion Muhammed Ali stated,

"Champions aren't made in the gym. Champions are made from something they have deep inside them – a desire, a dream, and a vision. They have to have last-minute stamina, they have to be a little faster, they have to have the skill and will. But the will must be stronger than the skill."

There are certainly many great men that have blazed the path of combatives, and they all deserve credit for their work. They have all been an inspiration during the development of these fighting concepts.

Gutterfighting - "Striking & B.E.A.T. Target Model"

We do not teach fancy striking techniques. I believe that anything will work when applying the B.E.A.T.(Brain, Eyes, Abdomen and Testicles) target model; however, here is a short list of some of the striking techniques that we use: Ax Hand (long/short), Face Smash, Chin Jab, Headbutt, Straight Blast, Cupped Hand Strike, Elbows, Hammer Fist, Knee Smash, and Shin Kicks.

We utilize the B.E.A.T. Model in application of all striking techniques. This model of striking application was adopted from Frank Albert's great book One-Strike Stopping Power – How to Win Street Confrontations with Speed and Skill. This book is available at www.paladin-press.com.

All striking techniques are applied to one of these target areas and are used to distract your adversary long enough for you to exit the threat zone or distract your opponent so that an effective take-down to controlling follow-up is applied. As you already know, these blows will most likely not cause an instant knockout but they will usually cause a great distraction. Striking these target areas will create a very short time period in which your adversary is not thinking about you, but instead his own pain. That is your window of opportunity. Dominate him! Do not stand around waiting for something else to happen. Use this window of distraction to your advantage and continue the fight until your adversary is down and out. You must fight "down and dirty." Do not give up until it is over.

Many years ago, Forrest E. Morgan wrote a wonderful book entitled Living the Martial Way. In his book there is a very interesting quote: "If someone asked me what a human being ought to devote the maximum of his time to, I would answer, 'Training'." Some might think this a little fanatical, but I would disagree. Someone also once said that "Proper Preparation Prevents Poor Performance." I certainly do agree with this statement. Remember as the warrior trainer, you must also set aside time each day to work on your own warrior skills; this is the only way that you will grow and win! What are warrior skills? Simply put, they are life skills. Anyone who adopts the warrior mindset and prepares the body properly can handle life's straight pitches as well as its curveballs.

So there you have it, the "Gutterfighter Way!" Prepare your mind, prepare your body, practice your physical skills and be ready for an all out battle. Hopefully the day never comes that you need these skills but if you do, BE READY! Train with a Gutterfighting mindset and practice all survival skills until they are second nature. "Train Today for Tomorrow's Battles."

Steven Mosley has over two decades of law enforcement experience. He is the Owner/Coach of Combat Hard Fitness & Fighting. He also serves as the Director of Training for Force One Readiness and the Georgia Tactical Officers Association.

In addition to work-related experience, Steven has over 20 years experience in martial arts and is an Apprentice Instructor in Filipino Martial Arts & Jun Fan Gung Fu under Guro Dan Inosanto. He is also a Senior Instructor under the British Combat Association and USA Director for CombatCoaching.com.

For more information, please visit www.combathard.com or contact Steve at: stevenmosley@hotmail.com.

TRAINING FOR THE REAL FIGHT

by Paul Howe

Realistic training for a future gunfight is critical for a successful outcome. My combat experiences have taught me to reevaluate my training system, work ethic and how to channel my training regime into a more streamlined and effective package. It also confirmed some lessons while voiding others. Proven combat techniques may not be flashy and may require a bit more physical effort on the part of the shooter. Further, they may not win competition matches, but they will help ensure your survival in a shooting or gunfight on the street.

First, I learned through experience that I would rather be in a "Shooting" than a "Gunfight." The difference is simple. A shooting is one-way event; I do all the shooting. The gunfight is where your opponent has the opportunity to fight back. I prefer the shooting to the gunfight as getting shot at leads to getting shot and this hurts.

You make it a shooting instead of a gunfight simply by seeing faster and anticipating the fight. It begins by setting yourself up in a tactically superior position before the fight happens. Further, equipment, physical conditions and mindset play critical roles in your success.

Vision and Scanning

One problem I generally see in LE training is that more emphasis is put on flat range fire rather than learning to see and discriminate faster, which are equally as important. I ask individuals if they see first or shoot first in a tactical situation? The answer is simple, you must see first before you can shoot. Seeing and processing the information faster than your opponent is the key to whether you are in a shooting or in a gunfight.

Scanning and discrimination drills should compliment your live fire training. I always suggest you look at the "Whole Person" and then hands in a tactical encounter to help prevent fratricide. This is especially true for active shooter response scenarios and multi-breach point operations.

Training

Into today's tactical community, several training vehicles for combat exist. They take the form of the LE academy, in service training and real world encounters. Other avenues that can be used are the IPDA and IPSC competitions and training. Even Cowboy Action Shooting (CAS) attempts to replicate a historical version of personal combat.

Beyond shooting, physical fitness is also critical to mission success. The better shape you are in, the less likely you are to get hurt and if you do get hurt, you will heal faster. I watch too many individuals today who rely on their weapon to solve all the problems. The problem is that you have to move that weapon to a solid shooting position not once, but multiple times during an engagement. This requires strength, stamina and endurance. Many folks do not have the physical conditioning to get to or stay in the fight.

Competition Versus Reality

Let's face it, competition is fun and if applied correctly, can help you in your marksmanship, weapon handling skills and confidence. With these attributes, also comes a bad habit of moving too fast for the tactical situation.

Who dictates the speed of the fight? The bad guy and how fast he falls, does. It might be a fast or slow process (the bad guy dying), but one should get in the habit of solving one problem at a time before moving to multiple threats. You can shoot two rounds on paper or ping a piece of steel and move to the next target, but in reality, two rounds or the sound of steel being struck may not solve your problem.

I remember servicing a bad guy one night at about 7 yards with night optics. I was trained to do double-taps throughout my military career. I punched him twice with two 5.56 rounds and stopped for a split second in my mind and on the trigger, looking for a response from the bad guy. The problem was that he was still standing with an AK-47. I hit him with two more rounds before he began to fall the ground. To my amazement, he stood back up before collapsing a second time.

Lessons learned, shoot until they go down. Not one, not two, or three. I now teach a five in the chest, one in the head failure drill with the rifle. Why five? It may take the human body that long to react to the amount of trauma you are inducing (5.56). At the time of this incident, we were using military green tip ammo and the energy transfer was minimal. Realizing we had a stopping power problem, we developed a drill that would work on any determined individual and made it part of our training package. I also teach this drill when using a pistol.

As a final point, I would be cautious on using competition shooters to drive the equipment and training in a department. While generally faster shooters, I have watched them err on the side of equipment that was great for competition, but took away from simplicity and the common goal. I remember arguing in 1993 for a more effective round for our primary weapon (rifle) as the 5.56 Green Tip was not doing well. Others soldiers I worked with, competed in weekend matches, were more interested in "square" triggers on the .45 for a uniform pull instead of the stopping power of their main battle rifle. We are still fighting rifle caliber problems today and sadly enough, service personnel have lost their lives because of it.

Equipment

As an assaulter, my body weight was around 230 pounds, but when tactically loaded with weapon, vest and helmet, it was closer to 310. This was simple assault gear and not a rucksack.

Fast moving raids require you to move efficiently and swiftly in, around or over obstacles with all your equipment. I have witnessed individuals packing their vest with excess ammunition or equipment that was a mental comfort item and not mission essential. This caused them problems in movement and fatigue.

Physically, you need to be able to move through an obstacle course with all your equipment to ensure that you can fight with your "combat weight." Also, you quickly find what stays on and what falls off. Make changes as necessary. If strength and endurance is an issue, get in shape. Hit the pavement, get in a gym or better yet, do both. If when looking in a mirror, you see yourself wearing overlapping gun belts, do something about it.

As for combat loads, look at how much ammo and how many weapons you are carrying. I have watched folks carry 12 to 20 magazines on their body and in my opinion it is too much. You cannot effectively maneuver with that weight nor sustain any aggressive operation tempo for any length of time. Generally 4-5 magazines in an law enforcement environment is more than adequate for any situation.

Let's do the math on this one. If you critically hit a bad guy with one out of three rounds you fire, that translates to 10 people per 30 round magazine. Carry five magazines and we are looking at 50 people you have critically injured. Multiply that times five officers on a tactical team and you have 250 folks you have neutralized. I think you get my point. If the situation becomes so critical that you need more ammo, you will have plenty of dead and wounded on your side that will not need theirs. If it makes you feel better, keep a few extra magazines in the trunk of your car.

Mindset

My firearm training began with a revolver and limited rounds. I knew that I only had six and that I had to make each one count. I developed a mindset of dedicated accuracy, even though I might be a bit slower than the shooter on my right or left. Additionally, my first formal training was with the FBI course of fire out to 50 yards.

This developed a sense of confidence that you could make a hit at further distances, if you did your part.

This mindset continued into my special operations career. Generally we were fighting an enemy who wore pajamas, carried an AK-47 and two magazines. They were on their own turf, acclimated and could run circles around you if you came to the fight too heavy. I would rather carry 7-8 magazines and be able to move and out maneuver the enemy than to be slow and sluggish and let them get into a better tactical position before I did. Also, if I shot my ammo wastefully getting there, no "ammo fairy" was going to bring you more one the shooting starts. So, I learned to be efficient with what I had.

The Fight and Setting Up Your Opponents

I push the use of cover to all my students. Brick walls and dirt stop bullets better than your Kevlar or "Chicken Plate." Many of the competitions that I have viewed or participated in have the shooter exposed to multiple targets during the course of fire. This is okay for the game, but if you overexpose yourself to multiple opponents, they can all shoot at you, where you can effectively focus on only one individual at a time. You loose.

Learn to engage/expose yourself to one threat at a time. Further, maximize the use of cover and minimize your exposure. Make the bad guy give you a full body shot to engage while you only give him your right eye and weapon. In short, make yourself a hard target. Most of the friendly casualties I observed were shot when they failed to use cover, or stopped in the open and not moving. This is also how I engaged most of the enemy that I know I got solid hits on. They were stopped in the open. I also had the chance to engage movers from a stationary position and within 100 yards, generally require a center hold for a solid hit.

In reference to shooting on the move; it is a skill that all shooters aspire to learn and spend a great deal of time and effort trying to master. I have never had to use it in combat. When moving at a careful hurry, I stopped planted and made my shots. When the bullets were flying, I was sprinting from cover to cover, moving too fast to shoot. I did not find an in between. If I slowed down enough to make a solid hit when under fire, I was an easy target, so I elected not to.

As for shooting and closing on a target, it only makes the bad guys accuracy better and walking into a muzzle may help you to test your new vest sooner than you wanted to. Diagonal movement works, but again if you have to slow down too much, you are an easy target, and are generally in the open. Speed can act as your security in this case to get you to a point of cover.

Key Points:

- Seek out instructors from both the speed shooting world and those who have been to combat. Select tactics, techniques and equipment that work for both, but lean heavily on the proven combat techniques. It may not be flashy, but it works.

- Always put in discrimination drills into your training.

- Train as you fight and with the same gear. During a shooting session with the team in all the tactical gear and ammo, take them on a short jog, O course or buddy carry and see how much gear they loose or if they can handle their own "combat weight."

- Solve one tactical problem at a time and then move to the next one, don't over expose yourself or sell the use of cover short.

Realistic tactical training may not feel rewarding at first. There are no prizes or medals to be had. The reward is being able to solve a deadly social problem quickly and efficiently in your community. The other reward is being able to go home at the end of the day and give the wife and kids another hug.

Paul R. Howe is a 20-year veteran and former Special Operations soldier and instructor.

Paul currently owns Combat Shooting and Tactics (CSAT) where he consults with, trains and evaluates law enforcement and government agencies in technical and tactical techniques throughout the special operations spectrum. See www.combatshootingandtactics.com for details.

TIRED OF "FEEL GOOD" TRAINING? CHALLENGE YOURSELF!

by Henk Iverson

Captain Hein B at last had a day off. Early morning, he decided to do some shopping at a local shopping center. As usual, he strapped his trusty Beretta 92F 9mmP onto his hip. This was a very wise decision as he would find out less than an hour later. Hein was not in the shopping mall for more than a few minutes when four men, armed with AK 47's, ran into the entrance.

One of the perpetrators fired a burst from his AK into the ceiling, screaming for the patrons to lie on the floor. Hein was in an isle, out of sight from the attackers. This was an armed robbery and the bad guys would not hesitate to use their assault rifles to escape. Hein drew his Beretta service pistol. He knew he had a full magazine on the gun and he had done a press check before he holstered, so his "arsenal" consisted of 16 9mmP ball rounds. He did not take a second magazine.

Now came crunch time, shoot or surrender. Being a member of a crack Reaction Unit, Hein was not about to give up the fight. He moved on the armed assailants. Cleverly using cover and concealment, Hein moved closer to the first bad guy, surprising him with a shot to the ribcage. The fight was on.

The armed robbers were caught completely off guard. There was somebody in this store, calm, trained and fighting back. A second assailant fired a long burst from his AK down an isle. Glass shattered and people screamed, but Hein was not there anymore. He had moved to another position to gain the advantage. He popped up firing two rounds at the second robber missing him, but drawing his attention. The gunman ducked down trying to shoot back, but Hein had already moved again.

The bad guys were now in disarray. They immediately tried to get out of the shop. Only problem was that Hein had moved towards the front door. They had only seen glimpses of him so far and he was shooting at them! Hein popped up again and fired several rounds at the now panicked and fleeing robbers. The robbers were trapped. Conserving ammunition, Hein fired three more rounds. He knew he had a clear field of fire as all the patrons were on the ground and he had a cement wall behind the bad guys. The bad guys fired wildly at where they thought the policeman was. The gunfight went on for nearly 12 minutes. Each and every time the bad guys tried to move, Hein fired a round at them.

By now the South African Police Flying Squad had arrived and Hein was really low on ammo. As the robbers made a break for the door, he let them escape from the store. Except for the wounded bad guy, nobody inside the store was hurt. This incident ended when the robbers hijacked a car, tried to escape and eventually rammed a police vehicle. More than 500 rounds were fired between the robbers and police officers. All four bad guys were killed. If you were trapped inside that store, could you handle a similar situation?

"Feel Good" Training

In the couple of years that I have been privileged to teach in the USA, I have seen a dangerous trend in the training arena that could get Law Enforcement Officers killed. I call this "feel good" training. We are so scared to hurt somebody else's feelings that we are willing to water down crucial training pertaining to officer safety. Let's sketch a picture to make a point.

A student attending pistol training will stand on the line, facing a paper target. The instructor will give the command to load. Now the instructor will give the command to fire. The student places his non-shooting hand in the middle of his chest, draws his firearm and fires the required number of rounds. Now he sweeps the target from left to right and then right to left a couple of times, "covering down" on the target. The student lowers the pistol into a 45 degree "low ready" position. Upon the command to holster, the student places his non-shooting hand on his chest and holsters his service pistol. Although most shots are on the target, spread all over, the instructor walks up to the student and says "Good Job!" Everybody, including the Chief of Police, the instructors and students all have smiles on their faces. This is "feel good" training.

If this was basic training and the student was a brand new officer, this type of training would be justified. The problem is that this is the current training trend in some police circles for ALL officers. Worse, the instructors calls it "gunfight" training!

What is the problem you might ask? If this is the training we offer our Law Enforcement Officials, how can we expect them to place their lives on the line to arrest extremely violent murderous criminals? How dare we expect an officer to enter a drug store and stop a machete wielding offender if the only training he/she has received was "feel good" training? Modern times are forcing us to change the way we think, the tactics we employ and the way we train. The year 2007 will go down as one of the most violent in terms of police injuries and deaths.

The time has come to change our training standards.

Core Skills

Change is always a challenge for most. Why change if it has been done for the last 20 years? This is where we have to pack away the ego and listen to facts.

Police Officers are being KILLED and INJURED by violent criminals in the execution of their duty.
Law Enforcement trends are towards less than lethal options. Pepper Spray and Tasers etc, are tools that are now in use on the street and these are good **OPTIONS** for officers. Let's look at what tools criminals use. When last did you see a gangster do a drive-by shooting with a Taser?

A lawyer puts a pen in his pocket when he goes to work in the morning, a doctor clips on his stethoscope and a law enforcement officer straps on a gun belt. Each one of these individuals is educated and dedicated. Only one of them has a gun as a primary tool to perform their duty. The lawyer saves lives with knowledge of the law and court system. The doctor saves lives with medical knowledge and skill. The law Enforcement officer walks the beat to serve and protect the innocent, yet who has the least hands-on training and who deals with violent criminals for a living? Fair? Police Officers **CREATE** a safe environment for the lawyer and doctor to work!

Officers work within arm's length of people. If we do not train them adequately to defend themselves from violent attacks at these close ranges, the likelihood of injuries and even death becomes a reality. Officers need core skills to effectively defend themselves at close ranges.

With that being said, what should officers be taught in a firearms training program? I call these CORE SKILLS. The foundation on which all other training is built.

Core skills should include but is not limited to:

- Basic empty hands strikes
- Re-active lateral movement off the line of attack
- Verbal engagement with offenders during the initial engagement
- Presentation of the duty pistol whilst under attack (without shooting yourself!)
- Finger off the trigger in a bent "C" position when not firing
- Accurate shot placement under duress
- Stoppage reduction (malfunction clearance) with tactical movement under duress
- Sustainability skills (magazine changes) with tactical movement under duress
- Retracted ready position after initial engagement
- 360 degree scans for more threats

These skills should be automated response for officers. We have to hammer it into them. When a pistol goes "click" in stead of "bang," the response should be: Finger into the "C" position, retract the pistol, move off the line of force, slap the bottom of the magazine to make sure it is seated properly, grab the slide over the to and rack with force, keep the muzzle on target at all times, back into the fight."

Integrate empty hands training with defensive firearms training. We cannot have one without the other. First the officer will need his knowledge of empty hand combatives to create an opportunity to get to other tools such as a duty handgun. I have seen it over and over where "defensive tactics" instructors teach their students to move INTO an assailant and the firearms trainer says create DISTANCE. Which one is the student to believe? Talk the same language!

Strong fundamentals – **CORE SKILLS** and **TACTICS** will pave the way for confidence in our officers.

Training For The Fight

Training should include something we call "tactical breathing." Tactical breathing saves lives. The important fact about loss of oxygen through decreased intake and the increased need for oxygen by the human body during life and death struggles, directly relates to performance under stress.

During the initial adrenal dump, the heart rate increases dramatically, breathing becomes fast and shallow which in turn will cause lack of adequate oxygen to the brain.

The brain will protect itself by shutting down blood flow to the extremities to make up for the reduced oxygen supply. Is this important to know? If you are shooting a pistol – **YOU BET!** Fine motor skills are diminished and trigger manipulation is such a fine motor skill.

An important fact that is mostly overlooked is that adrenalin creates strength in humans. Not important some say, but I can prove different. Most Law Enforcement training is done under controlled conditions. Under these conditions trigger pressure is a controlled act. Instructors encourage students to watch their front sight and put even pressure on the trigger to fire the gun accurately. With increased strength during a gunfight, the tendency to slam the trigger finger onto the trigger is greatly enhanced. Now add the loss of fine motor skills to the equation and we have a recipe for disaster. In layman's terms this means the chances of missing a crucial shot, even at very short ranges are very real.

There are many other things that your body will do to you such as the "tunnel vision" effect, loss of hearing, time distortion, and loss of depth perception. All have an effect on performance. To neutralize the oxygen loss to the extremities, we need to teach our officers to breathe properly during altercations. If your training programs do not include breathing under duress, your training is lacking crucial skills.

Breathe, Breathe, Breathe!
Train as if You Life Depends on it
– Because it Does!

Training should not be seen as a game. Train with intensity. Challenge students physically and mentally to perform under stressful circumstances. This means that we have to challenge officers to perform **BEYOND** what they **THINK** they are capable of. Leave the ego at the door.

There is nothing wrong with a little "tough love." Why are we so scared to fail a student every now and then? Set achievable standards, **HIGHER** each year. Train our people properly or do not send them out on the streets as a lamb to the slaughter! What is wrong with remedial training? Are we scared of admitting to an officer that he/she is not up to a specific task? The lives of our officers are too important not to be very serious about the training we provide. Why is it that the very best shooters in a Police Department are usually the firearms instructors? Easy answer, they get more range time! Shooting down steel plates does not prepare you for the violence of a gunfight. You may be the best shooter in the world but if you do not have the tactics and a "win at all cost" mind set, you might be killed in a gunfight.

Average shooters with great tactics and a winner's mind set make great warriors. Law enforcement officers need to be trained in tactics. To prevail, tactics have to be employed on a daily basis.

We have the opportunity to change from **"AVERAGE"** to **"GREAT."** That opportunity is still within our grasp. The street dictates if the training we provide is adequate. Training our officers should be our main concern. Challenge yourself to be the very best you can be. Your Country, your family and friends depend on you.

Henk Iverson served in the South African Military in a unique unit specializing in tracking terrorists on foot with dogs or visual trackers, on horseback and with off-road motorcycles. This unit was called the South West African Specialist Unit or SWASPES. After his military service, Henk joined the South African Police Service and was selected onto a Reaction Unit - a high risk SWAT type unit. The Reaction Unit's main function was counter terrorism. After 15 years police service, Henk started his own training company, specializing in CQB. Henk has worked all over the world and has protected the President of a country, trained special forces of several countries and now resides in the USA where he serves as the training director for STRIKE Tactical Solutions LLC. STRIKE Tactical provides Law Enforcement and the Military with the most modern fighting training available. www.striketactical.com

TRAINING ISSUES – AS I SEE IT

by Kelly Keith

Today, with easy access to information and videos relating to police assaults and shootings, law enforcement trainers and the officers themselves have no excuse not to be trained in and prepared for the most common ways in which officers are being assaulted and killed. What can be done to best train and prepare our officers for these assaults?

How is it that someone who is a 6th degree black belt in Karate comes into a Use of Force Class and shows one of the highest levels of timidity compared to the other recruits? I recall a student who came into one class and was downright cocky about his ability, and openly told anyone that would listen that he was a 6th degree black belt in Karate. When he was put through reality-based training where the role players hit, yell, and scream he folded his tent and became prey.

Just to set the record straight – I think Karate and many other point fighting arts are excellent activities and great exercises. However, this being said, a student who trains in these arts is NOT preparing him or herself for a real fight. To do this, one must use stress inoculation and be gradually exposed to the reality of a fight where punches and kicks are not for points but are for keeps. The fancy kicks and punches generally do not work, and there is no referee to stop and start things. I'm sure any of us who have went to the skating rink and played pick-up hockey know of many guys who were great at this type of hockey but could not duplicate those skills in true game conditions.

Some thoughts:

- Fancy techniques look great, but basic ones work. Complicated moves fall apart when someone is punching you in the face.

- Are your moves strength dependant? Strength dependant moves are great if we get to pick our opponents, however in the law enforcement world this is not the case. There are no weight classes, rules to prevent injury, referee's etc. in our confrontations. We must work on techniques that do not rely on brute strength.

- One size does not fit all – anyone who knows me, knows that this is my pet peeve. However, it is more often than not the way law enforcement officers are trained. This is wrong and does not stand the common sense or reality test in any way, shape, manner, or form. We must work on techniques that fit the individual officer's strengths and physical attributes and NOT the ones that the instructor is comfortable teaching.

- Do the techniques work on dynamic attacks or only when you have a compliant opponent who leaves his hand out after he throws a punch? Now, this being said, reality is also taken out the situation when the opponent is working on the same moves you are and knows what you are going to be doing so that he or she can block it. In a real fight you will never know what your opponent is going to strike you with. Steven Seagal wrist locks look awesome in movies but have you ever tried them when someone is not leaving his hand out or punching you with the other hand?

- Will your techniques work in real life environments? Law enforcement officers need to be comfortable working in small hallways, in vehicles, around tables, hills, snow etc. etc. etc. because in real life it is more than probable that this will be the environment that your confrontation will occur in. To win you must be able to adapt to all conditions and it cannot faze you.

- Are your techniques re-active to a specific attack method? Real fights generally have a flow to them that encompasses different ranges and different tactics. We have to get away from only teaching an officer to do one thing if the opponent does a certain attack in a certain way. If all you do is train this way, you are training to lose. Good fighters either consciously or un-consciously understand principle-based fighting, which is based around the principles of the different ranges and tactics. If an opponent moves his foot one way instead of another it may mean you push rather than pull or if the suspect is tired of punching and charges you - no big deal - the tactic just changed and so must you!!!

Another area that we need to take a good look at is gun and range training. We cannot mistake marksmanship training and training to win a gunfight as one and the same. This contrast takes us back to training to win a karate point fight as opposed to training to win a no-holds barred fight. There are major differences. It is absolutely necessary to teach fundamentals of shooting before gunfight training. However, at that point, our job as trainers is not complete. In marksmanship training the officer can stand still and shoot at a piece of paper, close one eye, and pull the trigger slowly. It is a fact though that the large majority of officers will not close an eye when involved in a gunfight. It is great to say that we can hit the target with an eye closed however if we know this may not occur in a gunfight we need to also train with both eyes open. If we stop our firearms training at this marksmanship level are we truly preparing the officer for the gunfight? Remember in a gunfight we are in a FIGHT. I suggest that standing still, pulling the trigger slowly, closing one eye while shooting long distances and hitting a paper target has very little similarity to the reality of a law enforcement shoot out and in fact may cost the officer his / her life if the officer training in this manner does not understand how to win that gunfight. This is even farther from reality than training the officer to kick and punch a bag. At least, a bag supplies resistance. If we stop our gun training at this marksmanship level we are indeed hampering the officer's ability to win a gunfight.

Before beginning any gun training I always ask the students: "Is it more important to hit your target in a gunfight or to not get hit?" Statistics show us that approximately 75 % of gunfights occur within 10 feet. It is a fact that law enforcement officers are generally reacting to a threat in a gunfight and not initiating it. If we are reacting, should we not be creating muscle memory to move laterally or tactically while drawing our handgun

– in order to either move to cover or if no cover exists than to move to make it difficult for the suspect to hit us? There are also times when it is tactically advantageous to move in a forward direction and to engage the threat. This should also be trained. The bottom line is that all officers should be comfortable moving while drawing and shooting. Moving laterally is a beneficial movement whether the object coming at us is a bullet or an edged weapon! Again, I want to stress that I believe we need to learn basics and I am a big proponent of those being taught. However, we need to ensure that we are training law enforcement officers to win a gunfight and not a marksmanship competition. Additionally, we need to have officers make it second nature to be aware of cover and barriers at all times. It is very common to see shooters who are good in marksmanship and not good in reality-based firearms training.

It is also a fact that most deadly assaults occur between 6 P.M. and 6 A.M. where there is limited visibility. We must also train our officers to be comfortable working in this environment. Tactics change if you have a flashlight in your hand or your ability to perceive threats is diminished. Firearms training needs to reflect the amount of time they are likely to be in a deadly force encounter in low light situations.

Most departments across North America have a minimum yearly firearms qualification and yet it is a fact that a large percentage of shootings occur during or right after physical altercations. It is also a fact that law enforcement officers get in far more physical altercations than firearm altercations. For these reasons it is just as important to have at least yearly control tactics training.

Two areas that we must keep expanding upon are tactical firearms and reality-based training. Reality-based training can stress inoculate the officer. This topic alone could fill many books however the one thing that I feel is too important not to mention is: do not allow the officer going through the training to die! Officers do not need to be trained in how to die. They need to be trained on how to first avoid getting into the gunfight and when it cannot be avoided – on how to win it. All officers must be trained to fight and win even though they may get shot or hit.

It is a fact that many officers in a gunfight have had to draw their guns while on the ground, in their car or while they were engaged in a fight. If for whatever reason an officer winds up on the ground and is in need of getting to his/her firearm it is imperative that he or she has been trained in and is capable of doing this. Furthermore, if we are going to train officers to draw and shoot their firearm from the supine position we need to ensure that the officer is comfortable in having his/her feet in the air while shooting in order to keep an attacking suspect back. If the suspect has an edged weapon, having the feet up in the air can give the officer the time to get his or her gun from the holster, fire the rounds to neutralize the threat and WIN! Do not think for a minute that the action of getting your feet in the air to keep the suspect back will come naturally unless you have trained! In a true dynamic fight you may shoot your foot, however if you do not have your feet up to give yourself the time to get to your gun, the suspect may get to you first or even while you are shooting.

We must also remind officers that a "one shot drop" is a myth or their hesitation after the first shot may also be the deciding factor in who wins and who loses the confrontation. We need to give our officers the time required to control the threat. This may take 2, 3, 4 or 5 shots.

The facts are that most of the officers killed are uniformed patrol officers, rather than emergency response team members. Emergency response team members have numbers, weapons and tactics generally in their favor. Due to the fact that most regular and deadly assaults upon law enforcement officers are spontaneous we need to need to train police officers to make spontaneous decisions based on limited knowledge. We need to elaborate on Colonel Boyd's OODA loop philosophy (Observe, Orient, Decide, and Act) in order to allow officers to get every advantage possible. Reading a suspect's body language and then reacting appropriately to these signs CANNOT be overlooked. In the majority of cases the suspect will show some sort of body language which will come before an attack.

As I mentioned at the beginning of this article - in today's world, with the easy access to information and videos relating to police assaults and shootings, law enforcement trainers and the officers themselves have no excuse not to be trained in and prepared for the most common ways in which officers are being assaulted and killed. Let's continue to improve in our training methods by utilizing good tactical firearms and reality based training.

Inspector Kelly Keith is a 20 year veteran of policing. He is an Inspector with the Atlantic Police Academy instructing Physical Fitness, Officer Safety, Use of Force, and Tactical Firearms. Kelly is a second degree black belt in jiu-jitsu (Bronze medalist at the World Jiu-Jitsu Championship, Vancouver) and has studied Wrestling, Boxing, Tae Kwon Do, and Judo.

He is also a Certified Personal Trainer, Certified Strength and Conditioning Instructor and a Certified Sports Nutrition Specialist.

Kelly can be reach by kkeith@pei.sympatico.ca or by phone: (902) 836-5277

FIT FOR DUTY?

by James Di Naso

One of the most important but often over looked questions a warrior could ever ask is: Am I fit for duty? While many warriors would answer yes, the real answer to this question doesn't come until an officer actually has to perform job related tasks and tactics that require physical skills on the street. Unfortunately, the answer comes to many warriors with a high price. Injury and officer death rates are on the rise and violence against police officers is at an all time high (National Law Enforcement, 2007).

Physical preparedness is one of the most important qualities a LE officer needs to develop to prevent injury and to win when it counts the most! Can you imagine going into battle with a group of unfit warriors who did not have the physical stamina or strength to adequately perform on the battlefield? But this exact thing is common place in the police world. Not only is it "acceptable" to be unfit for duty, officer perception, agency politics, union policies, political correctness, low standards, legal issues, and a lack of physical education have promoted a culture of physically unfit and unprepared police officers.

Are you prepared to handle the rigors and physical challenges that the law enforcement profession requires? Can you wrestle with a bigger and stronger offender for 2-3 minutes without extreme fatigue? Have you developed and practiced efficient movement skills so that you can use the handgun retention techniques and defensive tactics learned in training? Do you suffer from chronic low back and shoulder pain after sitting in the cruiser for several hours? Can you sprint 20 yards at full speed, negotiate obstacles and still shoot accurately while moving? Can you close or gain distance quickly to get out of the line of fire? Do you have the strength to drag a 180 lb person across an intersection to the other side of a street?

A true warrior does what it takes to prepare for all facets of the job, in spite of the culture. A true warrior facilitates change by example. A true warrior does not let officer perception, agency politics, union policies, political correctness, low standards, legal issues, and lack of physical education affect their preparation. A true warrior has the will to seek out solutions and prepare adequately! It is the intention of this author to challenge the minds of law enforcement officers to re-think the way they must prepare for the profession. This includes a fundamental paradigm shift in the way officers and police instructors think about physical training. The importance of being physically prepared and fit for duty cannot be overstated!

It should be understood that this is not intended to be an indictment of the law enforcement profession. I have come to these conclusions based primarily on my experience as a law enforcement instructor who has worked with thousands of officers at every level from around the United States. It also needs to be stated that many academies, agencies, and departments do a good job of promoting and cultivating an environment where physical fitness is emphasized and encouraged. Many warriors understand the importance of fitness training and put much effort into physical training. However, the majority of LE agencies and departments are way behind the curve when it comes to prioritizing and promoting officer fitness. A big part of the problem is the perception that officer fitness is a "small thing." Other issues seem to be more important and take precedence over such a "small thing" as officer fitness. Few would argue that workman's compensation claims, poor work performances, officer injury rates, officer fatalities, poor quality of life issues, and premature death rates after retirement are small things. Most administrators and officers do not realize that these issues can be, and many times are, directly related to an officer's physical fitness level. There also seems to be a wall of separation between the various disciplines with in LE training. It has been my observation that fitness training is not being integrated into a system that complements the defensive tactics and firearms training that officer's receive. This is very unfortunate because defensive tactics and other types of tactical training is only beneficial if officer's have the physical skills to effectively use them.

Shift work, stress, critical incident exposure, and long periods of inactivity punctuated by brief periods of intense, possibly life threatening activity are very demanding on the human body (Harvey, 2000, p. 16). But these are the requisites of the law enforcement profession. Job descriptions within the LE profession can vary, but listed are some of the most common physical tasks for a majority of those out on patrol:

- Quickly getting in and out of the cruiser
- Sprinting short distances
- Physically restraining offenders
- Baton striking

- Pushing stalled vehicles
- Carrying heavy firearms
- Breaching doors
- Crawling through windows
- Climbing multiple flights of stairs
- Moving while wearing a vest and duty belt
- Sitting and driving for extended periods of time

These physical demands of the job require adequate physical preparation. Thought and consideration must be given to physically preparing the body for the specific job related tasks of police work. Performing various exercises and workouts popularized in many bodybuilding magazines and fitness books are inadequate to prepare a warrior for the street. The human body adapts in highly specific ways in response to the type of physical fitness training imposed upon it. The important concept for all law enforcement officers to remember is this: "You get what you train for." Specific exercise programming = specific exercise results = specific impact on job related performance. If officers are going to spend time training, it is of the utmost importance that they perform exercises and follow routines that will have a positive impact on police performance! The goal of the physical training program should be to improve police performance and minimize risk of on the job injury.

These are some of the important physical qualities needed for LE officers to efficiently and safely perform on the job:

- Joint flexibility/stability
- Muscular strength
- Agility/speed/power
- Anaerobic endurance

- Movement skills
- Basic aerobic fitness

These physical qualities are the ingredients needed for what I call police specific fitness. **Police specific fitness is:** a type of fitness that enables an officer to perform all the physical skills, specific to the law enforcement profession, in a safe and efficient manner.

Police specific fitness:

- Increases the potential to win and survive violent physical confrontations
- Enhances the ability to perform job related technical/tactical skills requiring physical exertion
- Helps manage job related stress
- Minimizes the potential for on the job injury
- Improves self image and instills confidence
- Contributes to a higher quality of life

Here are two questions you can ask yourself to see if an exercise should be included in the fitness routine: Why am I performing the exercise? How will this exercise help my performance? Answers to these fundamental questions, or lack of an answer, can help an officer to assess whether the exercise routine needs to be adjusted or changed to be more law enforcement specific.

The following resources will be of great value to those seeking more information on police specific fitness including articles and Dartfish video clips of specific drills and exercises:

http://www.pkcotraining.com/Articles.html
http://www.pkcotraining.com/aboutme.html

The importance of being physically prepared and fit for duty cannot be understated! Officers need to understand the importance of police specific fitness and educate themselves on how to adequately physically prepare for the job in spite of the current unfit culture in the LE profession. The important physical qualities needed for LE officers to efficiently and safely perform on the job include: joint flexibility/stability, muscular strength, agility/speed/power, anaerobic endurance, movement skills, and basic aerobic fitness. Developing these physical qualities through training will improve police performance and minimize risk of on the job injury.

James Di Naso is co-owner of Police Kinesiology Company www.pkcotraining.com and serves as the company's Police Performance Director. Over the past several years, he has trained thousands of federal, state, county and city law enforcement officers. He has authored many articles on police specific fitness for various publications including Policeone.com and Law Officer Magazine. James is also an instructor for North East Multi Regional Training (NEMRT), a regional police-training academy in Illinois. James is a member of the International Law Enforcement Educators and Trainers Association (ILEETA) and has presented numerous times at the organizations annual conference. Prior to focusing his efforts on training law enforcement officers, James worked for seventeen years as a sports performance coach training athletes at every level including professional athletes from the NFL, NBA and MLB. He served as the Executive Sports Performance Director for Velocity Sports Performance in Willowbrook IL and owned and operated his own performance training business for fifteen years. James holds a Masters Degree in Exercise Science from Eastern Illinois University and professional certifications from the National Strength and Conditioning Association and the United States Weightlifting Federation.

References

1. National Law Enforcement Officers Memorial Fund and Concerns of Police Survivors (2007).
2. Harvey, B. Police Redondo Beach. (2000). 24(6). p. 16.

Warrior Reflections

"It is not the critic who counts, not the one who points out how the strong man tumbled or how the doer of deeds might have done them better. The credit belongs to the man who is actually in the arena; whose face is marred with sweat and dust and blood; who strives valiantly; who errs and comes short again and again; who knows the great enthusiasms, the great devotions and spends himself in a worthy cause and who, if he fails, at least fails while bearing greatly so that his place shall never be with those cold and timid souls who know neither victory nor defeat."

- Theodore Roosevelt

THE ELEPHANT IN THE CORNER

by Sergeant Jeff Baker

This article was originally published on www.policeone.com and is reprinted with their permission.

After 20 years in law enforcement, I thought I'd seen it all. I'd worked as a rural deputy sheriff, multi-jurisdictional narcotics task force detective, and police sergeant in a metro area of 800,000 people. I lost a friend and former trainee when he was ambushed and shot to death in his cruiser; I suffered through my partner's criminal trial after he stood accused of excessive force (he was acquitted). I survived two shootings in two years; rape, robbery, killings, child abuse, drug addled homeless, vehicle pursuits, the "Revolving Door of Justice," draconian policy from police administrators, a disconnect between cops and the public, and everything in between. Indeed, I was confident I had taken in just about everything one could reasonably expect to be exposed to as a law enforcement officer.

I was wrong.

On December 5, 2007 at 1342 hours, the entirety of my training and experience culminated in a single radio call that would forever change the lives of those involved.

Active shooter, the apex predator: a calm, deliberate and seemingly remorseless gunman with a high-powered military style rifle. Multiple magazines at his disposal, each brimming with ammunition capable of passing through concealable soft body armor. Unlimited places for the murderer to hide and a target rich environment full of civilians in a "gun free zone," a massive shopping mall of about 135 stores at Christmastime.

After what seemed like hours, the full magnitude of the horror was revealed to us: A dozen citizens shot, eight dead, two battling for their lives in area trauma wards. The 19-year-old suspect was dead from a self-inflicted gunshot wound.

As one of the first three police officers in the doors of the Von Maur mall that day, I experienced a wide array of emotions. Too often, we in the policing profession hiding our feelings about the sights and experiences we endure. Thankfully, in recent years the machismo has given way to a realization that Post Traumatic Stress Disorder is real. Officers involved in critical incidents are talking (and healing) rather than resorting to stuffing it away.

Two primary feelings I'll discuss here, fear and resentment, aren't terribly comfortable topics of conversation, but I believe the more honesty we bring to the conversation, the better prepared officers who follow in our footsteps in future incidents of this nature will be prepared to deal with them

Fear

I'm just going say it: Responding to this incident proved jarringly scary.

As the supervisor dispatched with district cars when the call was first broadcast, fear crept in that we would not get there in time — this despite a 100-plus mph response on a congested freeway leading to the mall.

My mind was racing as fast as my black-and-white: Is he still killing people? Will we make it in time? Will we be able to get to him before he hurts anyone else? What if he takes hostages? What if there are secondary shooters or explosive devices as there were at Columbine? What if a police officer goes down?"

Police are not soldiers per se, fighting a guerrilla enemy we cannot see, but this day was different.

I arrived and entered the store, scanning across the top of a 12-gauge shotgun loaded with rifled slugs. I fought the instinct to announce my presence as it has been ingrained in us to do. I couldn't afford to reveal my position to the gunman. In a breathtaking moment, two terrified citizens popped up and raced to me, then past and out the doors behind, tears streaming down their faces.

Everywhere I looked, I saw and smelled evidence of a monster on the loose: Store employees frozen under display cases; the first gunshot victim, mortally wounded, surrounded by 7.62mm shell casings; the smell of gunfire hanging in the air, reminiscent of the firecrackers I enjoyed as a kid.

Christmas music playing, eerily juxtaposed with the blaring fire alarm. I became conscious of my quickened breathing. Moderately asthmatic, I was puffing a bit as I relayed information on my portable radio to incoming responders.

Coffee cups, empty strollers and shopping bags littered the floors, abandoned at the spot people started to run. We formed up contact teams and incrementally cleared the mall, evacuating hundreds of shoppers and employees who had hidden themselves in some unusual places.

The shooting had been confined to one store, and had been committed by one suspect who was already dead. By the time the day ended some 13 hours after my shift began, I was completely spent, both emotionally and physically. So too were dozens of other involved officers.

Know ahead of time: Responding to an active shooter is unfathomably stressful.

Anxiousness can build with serious momentum during your response to the scene. The physical taxation your body is put under is exacerbated by this psychological reality. Your dedication, training, superior tactics, determination and sworn oath as a law enforcement officer will propel you through the barrier of the human instinct to run from — not toward — the sound of gunfire.

Thus, fear does not have to be the enemy of the police professional. Fear keeps you "on the yellow" and prepared to react with extreme prejudice when the Moment of Truth arrives.

Resentment

In all, an estimated 200 Omaha police officers made it to the scene, and untold more responded from outlying jurisdictions. Irrespective of agency, every "true-blue" cop I've talked to in the wake of this ordeal relays the same feeling of resentment that the shooter took his own life, unwilling to go head-to- head with the people equipped and prepared to meet him on the slaughter fields.

Admitting to outright anger over circumstances that did not allow us to deal a death blow to the suspect might seem macabre to some, but that's the world real cops live in. Make no mistake, we do not yearn for a call of this nature to erupt; but when it comes, we want to be there, to test our mettle against that of a ruthless killer, to save the lives of innocent people who pay our salaries or die trying.

This is not about martyrdom, it's about reality. The law officer is cognizant of the increasingly violent realities of the world, and while praying it doesn't happen in our hometown, we're sober-minded enough to accept the fact, given sufficient time, it probably will.

I encourage every officer to let that resentment go before it takes root and has a negative impact on the way you do your job.

After the Incident

If left unchecked, officer involvement in a critical incident can have serious health ramifications — think of dangerous coping mechanisms like binge drinking and other destructive behavior.

Personally, I found healing in department-provided CISD debriefing, in council with my priest and spiritual director and in prayer.

If you're into strength training or running, stay on your workout schedule. If you're not, start. My time in the gym was critical to the "decompression" process. Surround yourself with loved ones — your support network — and be willing to fellowship with your brothers and sisters in arms. You may never know the positive effects of giving a hug or slapping someone on the back and telling them you're proud of the job they did. We all need a little bit of affirmation at times.

Remember, dealing with an active shooter and multiple causalities is more than the tactical X's and O's of search teams, room clearing and victim evacuation. Emotion, the elephant in the corner for us cops, is something you will invariably deal with, both in real time during the incident and moving forward after the dust settles.

Be prepared when the wolf comes. Accept the anxiety, sadness and confusion that can come in those dark moments. Knowing ahead of time to brace yourself against images and impulses you may never have experienced — at least at this level — may be the difference between successfully managing the incident as your own mental wellbeing in the aftermath.

Sergeant Jeff Baker is a veteran of 20 years in law enforcement and is a past recipient of the Omaha Police Medal of Valor for his actions in a shootout with armed robbery suspects. He is the former editor of The Shield, the official publication of the Omaha Police Union, Local 101. He enjoys his Catholic faith and strength training, and is blessed in marriage to his wife, Denise. Sgt. Baker can be reached at opdsgt@gmail.com

THE SURVIVAL TRIANGLE

by Alexis Artwohl, Ph.D.

Behavioral science is relevant to how people operate and make decisions under stress, how perception and memory work, and psychological issues relevant to training and investigations. This comes most sharply into focus when officers use force against suspects, especially deadly force. This article addresses some of the "big picture" issues I've noticed that are relevant to use-of-force incidents.

Acting like a superhero

This was one of the big pictures I noticed first: It's surprising how many people think you should be a Robocop. When I first started doing debriefings with officers involved in shootings, I saw very clearly that police officers were often expected to not only defy the laws of physics and exceed the limits of human performance, but they were then held accountable and sometimes punished when they failed to achieve the impossible. It seemed that officers everywhere were expected to have unattainable traits, like the ability to see and hear everything, have perfect memory, demonstrate superhuman reflexes, be able to foretell the future and read minds. Among those who demanded these impossible qualities were the public, which one might expect, but also police staffers including the officers themselves.

As I looked into this further, I realized that many people both inside and outside of police work were uninformed about some basic physiological and human performance principles that had already been elucidated by behavioral science. To further complicate matters, it appears that relatively little research was being done on human performance factors specific to the daily work demands of police officers patrolling the streets. This meant that the training and judging of officers was often being done in the absence of any scientific foundation that would answer the important question: "How do you know what you think you know?" Not surprisingly, this leads to errors in training, investigations, policies and procedures. Recent research specific to the dynamics of police shootings has revealed some surprising findings.

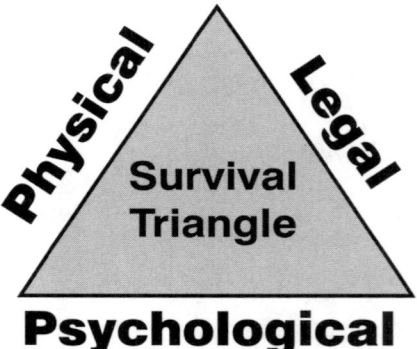

The Survival Triangle

Another big picture concept in the area of use-of-force is what I call the "survival triangle." There are three areas of survival officers need to be concerned about: physical, legal and psychological, and they are all intertwined with each other.

Physical survival: Although one officer line-of-duty death is too many, fewer police officers are now being murdered on the job than in years past. Tragedies such as the CHP Newhall shootout in 1970 and the FBI Miami shootout in 1986 forced law enforcement to pay closer attention to human performance factors in the training. The gratifying result was better training, resulting in fewer officer deaths.

However, there is still room for improvement. One example is the ongoing debate about the best firearms technique in a police gunfight — point shooting or sighted shooting. I always ask the question: "What does the research show works best on the street?" The frequent answer is "What research?" Fortunately, studies are now being done that may definitively answer questions like: Which technique is best for the average officer? For a more highly trained tactical officer? Does it make a difference how many hours of training the officer gets? Will training translate to behavior during an actual gunfight? How about lighting conditions?

Close attention to human performance factors and behavioral science research can help answer these and many other important questions.

Quadruple Legal Jeopardy Survival

There was something quite odd I have noticed about police work. Police officers are told it is their mission to protect the citizens from violent offenders. Since these violent offenders have a tendency to be, well, violent, the community and the agency equip officers with a variety of non-lethal and lethal use-of-force weapons and tactics to get the job done. Then, if the officer needs to deploy these use-of-force weapons and tactics that have been provided and that he has been trained on, an odd thing happens: he becomes a suspect in felony crime. So simply by virtue of doing their job, officers have to endure the investigative process as a suspect.

Police officers possess a tremendous amount of power. They can deprive citizens of their freedom and even their life, based on the individual judgment of the officer(s) within the scope of the law and the directives of the agency. With that power comes an equal amount of accountability, so the investigative process is inevitable. However, just as any citizen should expect a fair, non-politicized and fact-based investigation, we should grant the same right to officers without rushing to judgment or basing our conclusions on assumptions instead of scientifically-based facts.

In addition to officers undergoing a criminal investigation, they also face an internal affairs investigation to see if discipline and/or termination are warranted. It doesn't stop there, though, as agencies can also face civil litigation and federal civil rights charges. Behavioral science and human performance research is vital in helping the investigators, prosecutors, juries, the media and other members of the community understand the dynamics of use-of-force situations so the officers can be fairly and scientifically judged on their performance.

Psychological Survival

Many police officers have told me that dealing with the aftermath of an officer-involved shooting is more stressful than the shooting itself. This includes dealing with community reaction, media coverage, family concerns, fellow officers, agency rumors, and how they are treated by command staff, investigators, district attorneys and all the other stakeholders in the event. Helping officers in the aftermath is an important and complex area that is being explored and refined by behavioral science.

In the old days, officers were supposed to be in denial of the negative psychological impact brought on by use-of-force incidents. Just go to "choir practice" after work and get right back on that horse. Then there was a phase when it was thought that many officers would automatically be psychologically shattered and their careers destroyed if they were involved in a shooting. Not surprisingly, behavioral research is showing us the truth seems to be somewhere in between, and it is clarifying what might be done to help officers thrive in the aftermath of a critical incident.

Logic and Reason May Go Right Out The Window

Another big picture issue is our delusion that we are creatures of logic and reason. Research shows that much, if not most, of our decision-making is based on emotion and influenced by mental processing that we are not consciously aware of. This can be particularly true when decision-making is influenced by stress.

All the people involved in use-of-force incidents, including the suspects, cops, witnesses, community members, investigators and others are fallible human beings who are not possessed of perfect memories, infinite reserves of wisdom and restraint and impeccable logic. Add into this mix politics, opportunism and the personal biases and prejudices of all the humans involved, and the aftermath of a use-of-force incident can quickly become a three-ring circus. This tendency toward irrational behavior cannot be eliminated, but it's helpful if we acknowledge that emotion, bias, perceptual and memory distortions and subconscious motivations can influence the behavior of all the stakeholders and take that into account.

The Responsibility Triad

There are three entities involved in police use-of-force incidents which I call the "responsibility triad": the community, the agency and the officers. These three entities are a family, whether they like it not. They are stuck with each other and bound up in a complex, highly politicized and often emotionally charged relationship.

Like all family members, each has areas of rights and responsibilities within this relationship. Who is responsible for what may not be clearly defined, understood or agreed upon. For example, when a police officer is forced to shoot a homeless mentally ill person, who is responsible? The officer who is faced with a split-second decision? The community, who may not provide adequate funding for mental health centers? The legislature, who has passed laws that the mentally ill have the right to live on the street and refuse medication? The agency, which may not provide maximum training for officers on how to deal with the mentally ill? Academia, who may not provide adequate research on how this tragic situation of the homeless mentally ill should best be handled?

Obviously, no one entity is responsible, but sometimes that can be overlooked when a shooting makes headlines and it is the officer who comes under scrutiny. This does not absolve the officer of responsibility for the shooting, but acknowledges that the shooting was the culmination of a long sequence of events involving many different entities and areas of responsibility.

When there is high profile use-of-force case, the stress level of all three entities can skyrocket. Like all families under duress, the pressure can seriously strain relationships and both individuals and groups can operate in a manner that seems to defy logic, because it often does.

Under this intense pressure, hopefully the community, agency and officers will have made enough deposits into their joint bank account of goodwill and understanding to get them through the big withdrawals that will be made during use-of-force incidents. Educating community members about the science of police work is critical, but the emotional element of winning hearts and minds is equally important.

People Who Need People

Police work is primarily a people business. A limited amount of time is spent fooling around with equipment and other impersonal tasks. The job is intensely involved with human beings. You are out there because your community needs you to protect them from predators, you need your fellow officers to help you and watch your back and you need your agency to provide the training, equipment and leadership to get the job done. All of this requires a great deal of interaction with people in all aspects of your career. Whether you tend to like people or not, you will be much more effective if you learn what makes them tick and find positive ways to interact with them that will allow you to accomplish your goals.

From time to time I work with officers who have become so aggravated and worked up over these interpersonal tasks that they wind up in therapy. They complain bitterly about politics and those who "play the game." When I ask them to define politics, they often list negative behaviors, like "brown-nosing." I ask them if they would consider an alternative definition of politics: "The ability to understand and get along with others so you can positively and successfully negotiate for you want." We then discuss how a huge portion of their job involves that task, and how it is a good idea to become more competent at it instead of just complaining about what a pain it is.

Behavioral science provides insights in this area. There are many books and training opportunities available that can provide officers with better interpersonal skills so they can see getting along with others in the community and their agencies as an interesting and rewarding challenge instead of something to feel bitter about.

Nobody's Perfect

So, as it turns out, not only are you not a Robocop, but all the other people you interact with aren't perfect either. Given the influence emotion has in our decision-making, we sometimes like to indulge ourselves with the fantasy that we are the perfectly logical ones and everyone else is being unreasonable or downright nuts. Plus, of course, our memory and opinion of an event is perfect and it's the other person who is seeing it all wrong. However, on the emotional side, a little understanding, empathy and willingness to not rush to judgment can do us all some good and maybe get us a step closer to looking at reality. On the logical side, behavioral science can help us better understand that reality. Getting a handle on the incredibly complex task of police work and understanding use-of-force incidents is a daunting task and obviously will always be a work in progress with much to be learned.

This article first appeared in the Summer 2007 issue of The Tactical Edge, the quarterly professional journal of the National Tactical Officers Association.

Dr. Alexis Artwohl is a behavioral scientist who does training and research in the area of the psychological issues relevant to police use-of-force.

She can be contacted through her Web site at www.alexisartwohl.com.

THE C-ZONE OF COMBAT PREPARATION

by Lt. Harvey V. Hedden (Retired) - Kenosha County Sheriffs Department

It was only a practice game for a recreational softball league. In order to maximize participation, every child on the team took the field. My son was assigned to deep left field where eight year olds rarely ever hit a ball. As the game progressed, the routine of inactivity created complacency. The game was the last thing on his mind as he examined the shapes of the clouds and watched nearby ants at work. When the ball came rolling through the grass, it should have been easy to retrieve if he had been prepared, but the OODA (Observe, Orient, Decide, and Act) loop worked against him and the ball rolled on by. As a result an extra run scored. His pride was a casualty and for at least two full innings, he tried to focus on the game. As the day wore on boredom returned, but fortunately, no softballs did.

Preparing law enforcement officers for combat faces similar challenges. Routine tasks and calls for service, long periods of inactivity and everyday distractions all work against the officer. It's easy to forget that we may have to take the life of another or that someone may try to take ours just because of our occupation. More than 99% of the time we use almost no force at all. Of the remaining less than 1%, deadly threats are a rare occurrence. It is very difficult to stay on guard for that threat which seemingly never comes. But in law enforcement even a few moments of complacency can have permanent consequences.

When an offender is confronted by a law enforcement officer he has five alternative courses of action. The most preferable to us is surrender. But a suspect unwilling to face imprisonment may at least initially attempt another course of action. He may attempt to negotiate with the officer in the hopes of avoiding arrest by convincing him he has the wrong person. He may attempt flight to elude the arrest. He may choose to fight with the officer including the use of deadly force. Finally, he may choose to self destruct with suicide by cop becoming a popular option.

People who kill law enforcement officers do so most often because they perceive the officer as a barrier to something they want, usually freedom. They may be mentally disturbed or have coldly calculated that if an officer gets in their way, they would kill him/her. This decision is based on an appraisal of the likelihood of a desirable outcome by assessing the strengths and weaknesses of each side. Many officers die unaware that such a process is underway because they are unaware that any threat exists. Awareness actually dissuades an attack because we take steps to maintain control and advantage over our adversary. Interviews of both actual and would be cop-killers who surrendered to officers support this view. Our responses help determine an offender's choice and work to possibly avoid the deadly force encounter altogether.

For those offenders who misjudge the tactical situation or would rather go out in a "blaze of glory," we must be prepared to fight. A cursory analysis of armed confrontations reveals that the shooting problem is usually a short range transaction not requiring exceptional marksmanship. Having spent considerable time and money early in my career to prepare myself to use a firearm defensively it became clear that the firearm is but a tool and the real weapon will always be the mind. Situational awareness, tactical planning and the ability to employ defensive skills under pressure are key elements of mental preparation for combat.

At this same time I became familiar with the works of Tom Peters, Wayne Dyer, Dennis Waitley and other experts who work in the field of performance psychology. Dr. Robert Kriegel coined the term the "C-Zone" in his lecture, Power Under Pressure, to describe key elements for high levels of performance during periods of stress. When I began teaching officer survival in the early 80's, I adapted many of these concepts to create a C-Zone of combat preparation.

Competence

Traditionally, preparation for combat includes mastery of physical skills with a variety of equipment under conditions that approximate field situations. We spend many hours at the range and attain certifications in weapons such as the TASER and pepper spray. Far fewer hours are spent on the legal standards of use of force and our department policies. Under stress these inadequacies can cause confusion and delay. They can cause the officer to use excessive or more often inadequate force. Competence should therefore be balanced between the how to use and when to use disciplines.

Confidence

Believing in self sounds easy enough, but confidence has to be based upon real experience and personal history. Preparing for combat is not unlike preparing for a football game. First, we must understand the nature of the combat and the rules of the game. Next we develop mastery of physical skills. We must then learn to coordinate our efforts with others on our team into a cohesive plan of action. Finally, we must practice through structured role play and evaluate our performance for potential improvement. It is through experiential training that real confidence develops. As we develop our own personal highlight memory bank of past successes, we also create a database of potential solutions to future real tactical problems. This process continues on the street as we meet and resolve new problems and continue to build our mental library of experience.

Commitment

A common error made by both individuals and organizations is to believe that they have achieved the highest level of proficiency and that no further study is required. There have been many historical examples of law enforcement agencies who believed they were the well spring of knowledge from which other less enlightened agencies were allowed to drink. While they admired their accomplishment, the remainder of the law enforcement community continued to evolve and surpassed them. We must forever be a student, constantly challenging ourselves to improve. The best law enforcement trainers I have known were always more interested in what their contemporaries were up to than seeking accolades for their own brilliance. Commitment should also include honest self appraisal after each training session or street incident to help us learn from our successes and errors.

You must also commit yourself to winning. In a life or death confrontation, the winner is often the one who wanted it more while the loser gave up. As long as you are conscious, you must continue to fight, using whatever resources to which you may avail yourself. The majority of gunshot wounds are not fatal, but many people die from the shock induced by their own reaction to trauma. During the Second World War, there were many cases of what became known as "Surrender Death." Facing an overwhelming Bonzai charge, some soldiers were found dead without any serious wound. It is believed that they shut themselves off to avoid what they believed to be an inevitable, painful death. Conversely there are many accounts of persons who suffered what pathologists would judge as a non-survivable gunshot wound and not only lived, but won the fight.

Courage

It is not the absence of fear, but the ability to perform in spite of fear that defines courage. We tend to fear that which we do not understand. Through experiential training we can develop understanding and situational dominance. When we understand better the nature of threats, we determine methods to counter them thereby reducing potential fear. Positive self talk can help us focus on the task at hand and displace fear.

It is not courageous to risk our life for little gain. Television mythology would have us believe that officers must risk their lives to catch the bad guy. Is it cost effective to risk the life or health of an officer to stop a criminal whose act will cost the community less than even a temporary loss of the officer? It is for this reason than many agencies now discontinue misdemeanor pursuits when it is clear that the risks outweigh the benefits. When officers consider putting themselves at risk they must ask what is the potential risk of the suspect's escape vs. risk to self, other officers and the community.

Conditioning

Just as we must condition the body and prepare it for the stress of combat, the mind needs exercise in solving tactical problems, sometimes called crisis rehearsal. For decades athletes have used mental visualization to prepare for competition. A critical component of such conditioning is the ability to determine objectively reasonable force options. Delay in this decision can put the officer at significant disadvantage. Using too little force is more common than excessive force and can result in the need for more force repetitions and potential injury for both officer and suspect. These mental exercises can be as valuable as actual street experience. Planning for potential suspect actions and responses during actual incidents also reduces reaction time. Relaxation techniques such as autogenic breathing can help return the brain to better operating conditions during stress.

Communication and Coordination

Law enforcement has tremendous potential for reinforcements which allows for adequate time to coordinate an effective response. Coordination of work is key to the effectiveness of any organization, but too often our tactical training is directed at a lone officer. It is not surprising to hear officers attach adjectives which include the word cluster anytime large numbers attempt to solve a tactical problem. If members of a football team practiced as individuals and never scrimmaged, how effective would we expect them to be on game day?

Knowledge is power and law enforcement officers today have incredible access to information through mobile data computers, access to databases from other agencies and the internet. We should not overlook the importance of the dispatcher in providing vital information from persons at the scene to responding officers. When we know more about our adversary and the environment, we can better plan our response.

Interpersonal communication skills can often resolve confrontations with emotionally distraught persons. Foremost among these skills is empathetic listening and mediation. When it is necessary to speak, a calm commanding voice can help reduce anxiety of a person in distress as well as other officers.

Control – Time

Officers are frequently asked to increase their productivity, doing more work with less. But too often we adopt a time clock mentality in responding to high risk calls. Once a situation has been contained, time is one of our greatest resources. It allows us to better plan, gather and coordinate our resources. The same is not true for our adversary. Given enough time the offender will often realize his situation is hopeless and opt to surrender.

Control – Distance

Maintaining distance provides us more time to react to an offender's actions. It can permit a better overview of the scene and other potential threats. If a gunfight ensues, distance favors the better trained. In confrontations over seven yards in which both officer and offender are armed with handguns, the officer is almost always more effective in delivering accurate fire.

Control – Cover

Officers that move to cover at the onset of a gunfight are more likely to survive and win the confrontation. Cover allows us to reload, clear malfunctions and evaluate. In addition to becoming more aware of potential cover, we must practice overcoming an offender's cover through outflanking and over penetrating. One cover resource we can always take advantage of is body armor. Since its invention by Richard Davis, no other technology has saved as many officers from death or injury.

Control – Concealment/Detection

It is often advantageous to conduct a stand off reconnaissance prior to arrival at the scene of a call. Most officers wear a uniform and operate a marked squad car. In spite of this visibility, it is possible to reduce the opportunity for the suspect to detect our presence on the scene. Using binoculars, we can often see them before they see us. Excessive use of lighting tends to give away our position. Uniforms typically are adorned with badges, nameplates and buckles that reflect light. Noise from portable radios, squealing tires and footfalls also tend to give us away.

Control – Equipment

There are so many intermediate force options available to the officer today that a very real concern is the delay in deciding which one to employ. More options mean more training, more certifications and re-certifications. Just finding space on the gun belt for additional equipment is a challenge. Any defensive equipment on the officer's person must be easily deployable and yet well secured. A quality holster will not only allow for a fast draw, but enable the officer to quickly secure his handgun when it is not needed.

We tend to overlook the importance of quality footwear and gloves for the glitz of guns and combat knives.

Control – Self

Proactively maintaining situational awareness requires self discipline. Control of our emotions, most notably anger can help us avoid a fight. Regular sleep, good diet, preventative health and exercise all contribute to success in combat and longevity. The nature of our work does not make such mind-body harmony an easy task. Problems at home, frustration with our employer and financial concerns are but a few of the stressors that can distract us on the job. Stress itself kills many more officers than bullets. Each year many more officers kill themselves than are killed by others. Stress related diseases, alcohol and substance abuse will take others lives more slowly but just as certainly.

Although sometimes stress is unavoidable, we should never think we have to give in to it. Instead we should do what we will do on the street when something threatens our lives, fight back. Fortunately there are a wealth of resources just a Google search away to help us develop defenses, coping strategies and relaxation techniques to both reduce and manage stress. Professional counseling has lost much of the stigma it once held. Law enforcement is not for everyone. A career change may be preferable if a remedy to stress cannot be found. I have personally found relief in laughter, writing down my worries, recreation, faith and caring friends outside the job.

Conclusion

One of the old maxims of performance psychology is that "you will become what you think about most." If you commit yourself to prepare for combat and focus on that goal, then you will make whatever adaptations are necessary for its achievement. The concepts listed here are only a starting point for such preparation. Technology, most notably the internet with its vast availability of information has been a boon to law enforcement training and the evaluation of ideas. The ability to exchange thoughts with persons around the world provides us with a unique opportunity to share our ideas, challenge concepts and to develop new training and tactics that can help officers stay alive.

Dedicated to the memory of Deputy Frank Fabiano Jr., End of watch, May 16, 2007.

About the author: Harvey Hedden is a 26 year veteran of law enforcement and currently holds the rank of lieutenant with the Kenosha County Sheriffs Department. He is the field supervisor for the Kenosha County Controlled Substance Unit and heads his department's Marine Unit, Dive Team and Hostage Negotiation Unit. He holds a B.A in political science from the University of Wisconsin-

Parkside. Harvey has been a trainer for over twenty two years specializing in the areas of use of force, firearms, pepper spray, investigations and vehicle contacts. He is the Deputy Executive Director for ILEETA and a member of IALEFI, NTOA and the Wisconsin Narcotics Officers Association where he has served on their board of directors since 1990.

AMBIGUOUS RULES OF ENGAGEMENT AND THE FALLACY OF THE GREEN LIGHT

by Brian K. Sain

Ron McCarthy's timeless article "The Command Decision to Shoot a Hostage Taker: How Do We Make It?" appeared in the 1989 winter issue of The Tactical Edge. It is the author's opinion that the article should be chiseled into the side of a mountain somewhere and every aspiring tactical commander should be required to make a pilgrimage there to read it before assuming command of a team. The points Mr. McCarthy presented are as valid today as they were the day the article was written.

It has been roughly forty years since SWAT teams first appeared on the scene in American law enforcement. While researching this article I spoke with Mr. McCarthy briefly and informed him of some of the incidents mentioned in the following pages. He commented "Although forty years have passed, we are still apparently doing stupid things." He stated the only explanation he could come up with for this is because "People are people and some of them just have a really hard time doing the right thing." He went on to say "The snipers almost always get it right...it's their commanders that get it wrong." As usual, I found myself agreeing with him. But then...I am a sniper.

The American Sniper Association recently conducted a sniper utilization survey of every police agency in the

United States with 50 or more sworn personnel and a SWAT team. This effort took three years to complete and a survey form was completed on each agency. That is, each agency that would speak to the interviewers. Some agencies flatly refused to be involved. One agency stated they had never had a police sniper shooting at all when in fact; they had an incident go horribly wrong and they were trying to keep a lid on it. It is amazing how some agencies would rather save face than help someone else not make the same mistakes that they did.

Nevertheless, the results of the ASA survey are enlightening. Among the revelations was the confirmation of one thing we already knew. This being, the realities of tactical police work can be and often are...an ugly business. Bad things happen. Sometimes we can prevent them and sometimes we cannot. People do horrific things to other people. People also do incredibly heroic things and save other people's lives. People also make mistakes. These can be honest mistakes or mistakes of conscience; which brings us to the subject of this article.

In speaking with hundreds of police snipers over the years, many of them tell me the same thing over and over again. They say it is not the bad guys that cause them to lose sleep at night; it is their own people. Why is this so? I think Mr. McCarthy got it right in his comment that "Some people just have a really hard time doing the right thing."

I also believe this is because we as police officers know right up front where we stand with the bad guys and therefore train constantly to defend against them. But we never really expect our own command staff to betray us at the precise moment for which we have trained so hard to perform perfectly for. A moment we volunteered for but that they have ordered us into, to solve at their direction. Wondering if your commanders will back your play is distracting from the mission and is no way to operate. But unfortunately for some teams, this is what they must deal with on a day to day basis. The decision to take a human life is not an easy one to make for a peace officer; command staff or otherwise. However, for the police sniper, the decision needs to be made well before the sniper is suddenly required to act upon it.

Shooting a human being who may not be a threat to you personally (with the immediate results magnified in 10 power) is somewhat different than the more commonly encountered "It was either him or me scenario." Any moral or religious reservations need to be addressed beforehand so when the time does come, the sniper can act correctly under what is often a very compressed time frame. When the time comes for a sniper to shoot right now! … The time to decide if shooting is the moral thing to do has long since passed and lives literally hang in the balance.

If a sniper is suddenly placed in a situation where he has to fire his rifle immediately, the sniper will often have other issues to contend with such as suspect identification and isolation. Reaction time is crucial and the sniper needs to decide early on that "If the suspect does this…then I will do this." Sometimes referred to as "A mental line drawn in the sand," the decision has already been made and now the sniper only has to perform the required physical action to obtain the desired result.

This is a common thought process among snipers but often remains personal and unspoken. This is largely due to the fact that when spoken of in a matter of fact context to those that do not have the sniper's responsibility, and who have never spent any real world time employed as a sniper; voicing this process is sometimes misconstrued as cold blooded, heartless or even as ignorant machismo …even by other officers. The officers who feel this way do not really understand the mission of the sniper and usually have no real interest in learning. However, for the sniper himself, it is simply a mental process (much like a surgeon would go through before cutting out a malignant tumor) or pre-shot checklist that must be completed beforehand so the sniper can function as he is expected to within a fluid tactical environment.

For some of the more long standing teams and senior team members who have been there and done that (and anyone with any common sense at all), the authority to engage is a "no-brainer" SOP for both the snipers and their commanders. The only thing these officers have to worry about is getting better at their skills. Their confidence is visible and their teams…solid. The author knows of snipers who were involved in shootings, cleared of any improper action and were back to work in a matter of a few weeks or even days. This is the way it should be.

However, all too many teams still have to deal with self serving administrators and for some snipers, the antiquated green light methodology from upper level command staff who will do whatever they have to do, to remain upper level command staff. A Green Light policy, for the uninitiated, is the incorrect thinking that a police sniper must first request permission from a supervisor before he can fire his rifle in any circumstance, even in defense of life. This line of thinking is inconsistent with most use of force law and policy and is usually the end result of command level personnel making a feeble attempt to control a dynamic situation when they are really out of their capacity to do so. There is no valid reason that a police sniper, who should be one of the most highly trained officers and best marksmen in the department, should have to request permission to fire; whereas a rookie patrol officer just out of the police academy does not. There is just not enough time in a deadly force encounter to ask a third party's permission to fire and receive a reply before firing. Sadly however, there are still teams who operate this way.

Green light policies are often the result of pure self-preservation on the commanders' parts and dealing with this day to day is an uphill fight for the operators. The operators almost always know what needs to be done; but still have to work under ludicrous rules of engagement because of these people who have been placed in a position above them.

Trust between the two is non-existent and the operators are subliminally aware that that they will be "hung out to dry" if put in a compromising position.

Command personnel who institute green light policies are often driven solely by public/political opinion or their retirement plans and they do not need some SWAT guy "messing it up" for them. Some have the attitude "If a suspect kills someone; we didn't make him do it, therefore it is not our fault" These are often the same administrators who do not want to use the terms SWAT or sniper because both sound just a little too distasteful.

These same commanders will also try and negotiate with a suspect until the suspect runs out of beer, bullets and hostages to kill without lifting a finger to stop it. They seem to feel that police inaction and allowing the suspect to continue on, with mere hopes that he will surrender, is somehow acceptable; just as long as no criticism is placed on them or the department for reacting in what the public might perceive as being overly aggressive.

Having been placed in a position of authority, these commanders are often required to be on the scene of high profile incidents. However, when the time comes to make a tactical decision, these same commanders want to have a "rip cord" and the ability to "cut away" from and distance themselves from the operators if it all goes awry. These commanders will give ambiguous orders that can be loosely interpreted in case the outcome is anything less than positive. Being "in charge," they imply that they are advocating the use of deadly force by using some conundrum or code word but will not directly convey their wishes on the radio in plain language. This is so they have some "room" or "leeway" in the language used to distance themselves from the actual operators that took the shot, just in case the shot goes bad. I.E. "I said the suspect was not to leave the premises! I did not tell anyone to shoot the guy!"

Of course, despite their ineptitude, they will be right there to take the credit for a successful operation if it all goes well or as planned. For many of them, they are used to years of micro-managing the day to day goings on of a police agency and they attempt to use the same "management style" to "script" the response to a SWAT callout; instead of leaving it to the operators and tactical commanders who actually have the knowledge and fortitude to get the job done. Suspects do not care that the react team is not ready for the suspect to suddenly come outside or that the Chief has not arrived on the scene yet or any other myriad of variables which may occur on a callout and yet, these commanders try to exercise control over something they cannot control at all. No one can dictate what a hyped up suspect might do and teams are usually reactive in their response. But rather than adapt to the situation and act; some commanders are totally overwhelmed when the event does not play out the way they had "envisioned it would go" and the bad guy was operating on a totally different sheet of music. Green light policies and poor tactical decisions are by-products of this type of tactical management and often have to do with a commander's total lack of training or participation thereof. This can often be remedied if the commander will put in the time to train with his snipers. Many will not.

The sniper however, realizes all too well that anything can happen at any time. He is directly responsible for saving the people he can save, whenever the opportunity presents itself to do so and not when "the commander decides" that he is now finally ready for the sniper to act. To this end, the sniper cannot "think" he is doing the right thing. He must "know" he is doing the right thing and once he fires his rifle, he cannot call the bullet back. The sniper must know where his team mates are. He must know where hostages (if any) are located and he must know whether or not residences in his line of fire have been evacuated before he can fire a large caliber, centerfire rifle in an urban neighborhood.

If he has any doubt at all about whether or not the shot can be made successfully, with no collateral injuries, the sniper must err on the side of caution and he simply cannot fire. The sniper knows that if his shot is anything less than perfect, then the shot, and possibly the mission, will be a failure.

Ambiguous rules of engagement by commanders cause distrust, doubt and hesitation on the part of the snipers who usually believe, assume or hope the entire team and command are on the same page with them. The fact is: Sometimes they are on the same page and sometimes they are not and due to the fact these ambiguous orders often come right at the moment of truth...tragedy can be the result. The sniper team may pass on the only opportunity to end the incident which might have ever presented itself; while attempting to clarify exactly what the team's rules of engagement are and what is being expected of them by command staff who is supposed to be "calling the shots."

When snipers attempt to point these issues out to command staff, the often heard rationalization from their commanders is usually something similar to "I shouldn't have to tell you when to shoot someone and when not to"...Known as plausible denial, these commanders want the option to be able say "I didn't tell him to shoot anyone" or to have control so restrictive that it almost requires the Commander or Chief of Police to be right beside the sniper taking the shot when the order is given ...ala Green Light.

I offer a few cases here to illustrate the point:

A police sniper in the Deep South watches as a hostage taker escorts a hostage out of a residence and down the sidewalk to a vehicle on the street. The sniper has a clear shot at the hostage taker but the sniper does not fire. The hostage taker is allowed to go mobile and is stopped by another team member with a carbine who shoots the hostage taker through the vehicle glass, ending the standoff. The outcome was deemed successful but the entire team, (including the sniper) was furious. The rules of engagement (for the snipers only) of that particular agency restricted their snipers to the point that they absolutely could not fire unless specifically told to do so by a supervisor; even in the defense of life. The sniper readily admitted that he could have ended the standoff numerous times over before the situation went mobile but he was not about to violate department policy, which in his case was more restrictive than state law. In this agency, it was within policy for the perimeter man to fire without first "asking permission" but it was not so for the snipers.

In another case, fugitives on the run after a prison escape and the murder of a peace officer are believed to be hiding in a building which is surrounded by police.

A supervisor gives the order to all officers via radio that "They (the fugitives) are not to leave the building!" Snipers on the scene ask for confirmation that the men are to be engaged by rifle fire if they attempt to escape. The supervisor emphatically states "I did not say that! I said they are not to leave the building!"

In a very similar incident, a police sniper arrives on a rapidly evolving scene where a patrol commander is in charge. An armed suspect is attempting to go mobile with a hostage.

The patrol commander, who knows the sniper is there with his rifle, gives the order "The suspect vehicle is not to leave the scene." The sniper (who knows that the only absolute way to stop a motor vehicle weighing several thousand pounds with a 168 grain bullet is to eliminate the driver from the equation) asks for confirmation that the driver is to be engaged. The commander emphatically states "I did not say that! I said the vehicle is not to leave the scene!"

Another incident involved a Southeastern team who had a violent felon surrounded in a building. The snipers asked what the rules of engagement were and the commander emphatically stated that "The suspect is not to leave the premises!" The snipers asked for clarification and if this meant that they were to engage the suspect via rifle fire. The commander's reply was "Do what you have to do."

And lastly, a maniac brutally assaults his live in girlfriend, her mother and a small child. The female calls 911 and two patrol officers are dispatched to the disturbance call. The officers knock at the door and the suspect fires at them through it. The officers retreat, SWAT is called and a stand off begins. A police sniper arrives on the scene later than the rest of the team who are already deploying. As the sniper is walking to the TOC for his briefing, he asks the patrolmen what happened and the furious officers relay that they had been fired upon. As the sniper reaches the TOC, the sniper then asks the commander if this is indeed so and the commander states "We don't know that for sure" The baffled sniper then asks what the rules of engagement are and the commander tells him "Just go set up somewhere" The situation gets worse and the child hostage is later shot by the hostage taker. No useful information is communicated by command, before or after the child was shot so an informed decision can be made by either the entry/react teams or the sniper and the sniper subsequently demands to know what the status of the team is via radio. The sniper is immediately ordered to stand down. Believing there is a legitimate reason or pending tactical plan for this order, and per verbal (not written) SOP, the sniper repeats the order he is given to acknowledge that he received it. The suspect later surrenders and is taken into custody. In the aftermath, the commander attempts to place blame on the sniper for the hostage being shot but the commander is removed from command after taped radio traffic of the stand down order is brought to light. The former commander commits suicide on the third anniversary of the incident. It is discovered years later that the Chief of Police (whose contract was up for negotiation and who was actually at home but influencing the commander via cell phone) had told the commander earlier in the year "A bad guy may shoot someone here but that SWAT team is never going to shoot anyone" The well meaning operators on this team had no idea they were operating under these circumstances and had been beaten by their own people before they even arrived on the scene.

These are just five instances in which someone just couldn't do the right thing. It is not hard to see how these types of incidents can totally destroy morale and render a team ineffective.

However, sometimes you hear about a commander that does it right. In the Midwest, an intoxicated man with a military background and supremacist tendencies takes his wife hostage, beats her and tells her this is the day she will die. She escapes to a neighbor's residence and tells police the suspect is well-trained, armed with a stockpile of weapons and will kill officers if he gets the chance. The hidden suspect sprays fire indiscriminately around the scene, narrowly missing officers. The SWAT commander arrives on the scene and upon receiving a briefing, issues an order to all snipers that the first sniper with an unobstructed shot should take it. The suspect later walks out of the residence and points a weapon at officers and a sniper ends the violence.

Commanders like the one above know the law, are confident in their own abilities and are therefore confidence-inspiring to their team. Confidence breeds competence and we must have confidence in ourselves, our teammates and our administrations. All too often however, it is the latter that causes the problems. Politics have no place in the world of tactical operations and commanding officers must trust that their people are going to do the right thing when necessary. A team is a lot like a marriage and if there is no trust, then one is simply going through the motions.

A commander needs the inner strength to make the same right choices that he demands of his operators and he also needs to be supportive of his people and their decisions unless/until it is proven that their action/inaction or the consequences of either were improper in some way. A newly appointed sniper recently commented to me that during his basic sniper school, he had been instructed that "As a sniper, he would never be making decisions to shoot alone" He stated his Chief would always be making the decision for him.

This sniper is operating under the same needless restrictions as the operator from the Deep South mentioned earlier. So the "green light thing" just refuses to go away. Most readers here see the problem with this type of thinking but each agency has its own way of dealing with things. Some agencies intelligently address the issues head on. Others operate in blissful ignorance, totally unaware the issues even exist. Still others are aware of the issues but choose instead to ignore them with the hopes that "it will never happen here" or that they will never be the one's to deal with it.

In contrast to the new sniper mentioned above, the aforementioned sniper in the Midwest is an accomplished sniper. He is a combat veteran, has been involved in more than one shooting and no one needed to tell him the suspect needed to be shot. However, when his commander arrived, took control of the scene and let everyone know via radio that they were all on the same page (a team); it still made doing the right thing easier for everyone involved including the sniper, regardless of his operational experience. Needless to say, this commander is highly respected and more importantly, trusted by his men.

The author believes there is a place for specialized rules of engagement as they apply to snipers in tactical police work. The instances where they apply are limited. However, they do sometimes occur. A couple of examples:

There are times when a sniper should be told directly by command to fire upon the suspect(s) at the first available opportunity. An example here would be if the negotiators or command staff knows the suspect is threatening to kill or has already killed a hostage within a building but the sniper cannot see or otherwise does not know firsthand what is occurring. Command may (and should) give the order for the sniper to engage the target at the first available opportunity.

Command should relay in simple language what is transpiring so the sniper will be informed as to why he is being ordered to fire. But depending on the circumstances, command may not have the time to inform the sniper why this must be done and can only relay the order to fire itself. In this case, the sniper is just the mechanism for the command decision and implicit trust between command and the sniper element is imperative. The snipers must trust that command is making a proper decision and command must trust that the snipers will carry out the order they have given if and when the opportunity presents itself.

There are also times when a sniper should not fire his rifle under any circumstance. An example would be where a command to fire had previously been given but is rescinded because the suspect has now decided to surrender and command does not want the sniper team to engage him immediately upon sight. Again, command should explain why the order has now changed but simply may not have the time to do so if the suspect suddenly decides to surrender and goes for the door, unbeknownst to the sniper element that is waiting for him to re-appear.

However for the vast majority of callouts, and barring a specific circumstance or rule of engagement to the contrary, a sniper will usually deploy under the same use of force guidelines as any other officer in the department. The fact that the officer is armed with a sniper rifle alone should have no influence on the decision as to whether or not he is to use it to save a life.

Some other issues that need to be addressed are instances where snipers have been ordered not to fire their rifles, but did so anyway. If the sniper disobeys a direct order to stand down because the situation has now suddenly changed since the original order was given, only the sniper knows it and he does not have the time to relay this fact to command; the sniper very well may choose to take the shot and save a life. The sniper will certainly have to explain his actions later, but this just comes with the territory and is the proverbial "I did what I had to do" scenario and would be exactly the right thing to do under these specific circumstances.

There have been other instances where snipers followed their orders and did not fire after being ordered not to do so. I have heard people (who should know better) critique these snipers by stating things like "The sniper should have disobeyed that order and fired anyway." Statements like these often come from someone who has never been a sniper. It is irresponsible to make snap judgments on a sniper's performance without seeing exactly what the sniper saw, under the exact same circumstances the sniper was operating; at exactly the same time the sniper witnessed it.

A sniper makes decisions based on all of the information he has available to him at that very moment in time. It is ultimately his responsibility whether or not he pulls the trigger and he is responsible for every single thing his bullet touches along its flight path. If he has backstop issues, does not know where his teammates or hostages are located, etc. he simply cannot fire in lieu of making a bad situation worse. This fact is indisputable no matter what else happens or what he is forced to watch occur through his rifle scope. Disobeying orders, firing anyway and "forcing a shot" in this particular instance is a deadly roll of the dice. Proper personnel selection and training play a key role in preventing these instances from occurring.

If the sniper sees what he believes is a legitimate reason to fire, yet has to disobey a previous direct order NOT to fire to accomplish it, fires anyway and the shot is anything less than perfect (with absolutely no collateral injury to any person other than the intended target), the sniper will likely be indicted for a crime, with the penalty level thereof dependant upon the injury he has caused. Even if his shot misses his mark and causes no injury, the sniper will certainly stand alone, as the agency will not condone his decision in this instance. At the very least, the sniper may be removed from the team for lack of judgment.

Author's note: There have been instances where snipers "froze up" at the moment of truth and just could not pull the trigger. This is an entirely different subject for an entirely different article and one which this author is not qualified to write. But most often, a sniper either has a clear and unobstructed shot, under clearly established rules of engagement…or he doesn't…and whether or not he has the shot is usually the deciding factor in whether or not the sniper will pull the trigger. Again, proper training and personnel selection is the key to preventing tragedy.

Having a written sniper SOP in place can remedy many of the issues addressed in this article. The SOP needs to be written with input from the snipers themselves as no one better than they know the demands placed upon them. Rules of engagement and commands to fire need to be spelled out and given in plain language that are not subject to loose interpretation. All relevant supervisors should be issued a copy of the SOP and it will hopefully hold administrators to task. If and when the time comes when a sniper does take a shot, the agency can then say: "This is what we did. This is why we did it. We broke no policy or law." Furthermore, the SOP needs to address all issues affecting the snipers including specialized rules of engagement. If a sniper is currently operating without a written sniper SOP in place and terms like "rules of engagement" are a foreign language to his commanders and team mates, a sniper is better served operating under his agency's standard use of force policy just like everybody else. Trying to explain the issues addressed in this article for the first time, even to otherwise experienced people (who still may have no idea what you are talking about) can be a lesson in futility; especially if it is immediately following a critical incident. If an agency does not currently have a sniper SOP in place before a sniper shooting occurs, this gives someone an "out" and it usually isn't the sniper.

The job of the sniper isn't for everyone and it has been said that "the job finds the man and not the other way around." If you have volunteered for the scoped rifle assignment and can meet the challenges it brings... stay the course. The citizens and your agency need you ...whether they realize it or not.

Snipers needing assistance with an SOP or wishing to obtain a copy of the sniper utilization survey (available April, 2005), may contact the American Sniper Association via the website at www.americansniper.org.

Snipers may also consider joining Snipersonline.org and tapping into the collective knowledge of police snipers worldwide. Contact Lt. Keith Deneys at kdeneys@netnet.net to register.

Det. Brian K. Sain is a career police officer and police sniper in Texas. He is a member of the TTPOA, NTOA, IALEFI, ASLET, MMA, NRA (life) and is on the advisory boards of the American Sniper Association and Police Marksman Association. He is the Director of AmericanSnipers.org; a non-profit organization providing operational support to US snipers deployed abroad in the war on terror and may be reached via email at brianksain@yahoo.com.

THE ADVENTURE OF FOREIGN POLICING MISSIONS

by Assistant Chief David S. Butzer (Retired)

Looking for adventure after retirement or bored at your job? Can't see yourself in a rocking chair yet? Thinking about taking that winning attitude and mind out into the world, but don't want to switch to a whole different field? Maybe you want to do something important that can make a difference in the world and add some great stories to tell the grandchildren.

Well, think about this: work in a developing country and assist that country create, train and improve democratic policing or corrections. There are many ways to do this: provide direct or indirect law enforcement services in an emerging democracy; train or mentor public safety recruits and develop new local trainers; provide program supervision/management; provide personal security detail for dignitaries; provide site security; provide technical support to host country. This is only a partial list and there are many other options. Some key factors to success are your interest, abilities, and attitude. The W.I.N. approach and philosophy can help you succeed in foreign missions as well as at home. Most assignments require that you commit to a one year contract. Some agencies allow you to take a leave of absence for these international adventures, so this is not limited to retirees. However, the reality is that most of the contractors are retired or have quit.

My Story

Foreign policing missions can bring in a good income and the adventure of a lifetime. I truly enjoyed the majority of my time overseas and I do recommend it. Oh, the stories I have to tell. I even have the T-shirt to prove it! Let me tell the short version of my story and see if it appeals to you:

It the summer of 2003 my wife (Dr Alexis Artwohl) and I stopped to see a friend in Idaho and he told me of a training opportunity in Kosovo. In all honesty, all I knew about Kosovo was that it was in Europe and somehow connected to the Balkans. A small group of experts in community policing were headed there for a 9 week mission to conduct training in several small towns and cities. Spending nine weeks in an emerging European democracy training on a great topic with friends sounded intriguing and tempting.

I made contact with the coordinator and was invited to participate. Our team spent several weeks prepping for the course and getting our travel plans into place. Alexis offered tremendous support for my adventure, after all it was only nine weeks and I would be home in late November. I wound up coming back one year later from Baghdad but I'm getting ahead of myself.

I did some research and learned that Kosovo was controlled by Milosovich and the Serbians. The UN and Europe were actively engaged in creating a democracy in the disputed land, including the development of democratic law enforcement. Several nations contributed by sending police officers to provide a variety of police services, such as patrol, investigation and training.

The excitement grew as we arrived in Pristina, Kosovo. The airport was primitive and the initial ride with our hosts was most interesting. Poor roads, little traffic control, and clear evidence of a recent war added to the sense of adventure. The five of us spent the next nine weeks sharing four rooms in the house of local resident. We drove to the training sites thru some incredible country and met some wonderful people.

The one thing that sticks out in my mind was the enormous task the Kosovars' faced of interpreting democracy in their own way. The international community was supporting the philosophical transition to democracy, while the citizens struggled to imagine what freedom and democracy really meant to them. Does it mean you drive as fast as you want? Do whatever you want whenever you feel like it? What is the balance between individual freedom and the responsibility to respect the wishes and rights of others? How does a trainer explain the application and reality of democracy to a person that only sees it on TV?

The trip to Kosovo gave me a glimpse of what democratic nations can do to help those that need it the most. The chance to help a country to develop a professional democratic police force was very appealing to me. Kosovo was still emerging four years after the conflict had ended. The long history of violence in the region may be impeding progress, but the potential is incredible and worth the investment. One day I went into a grocery store in Pristina and was pantomiming to the owner what

I was trying to buy. Very few Kosovars speak English. He asked, "American?" A bit fearfully, I nodded yes. He then pointed at me and started yelling "American!" to the other customers in the store. Everyone smiled at me and started clapping, giving me an ovation. They are truly grateful for what the US and EU have done for them. I was hooked.

Here is what happened to transform me from a novice contractor to a "mission rat" with multiple missions under my belt: Shortly after arrival in Kosovo, I learned of an opportunity in the country of Jordan: the US was planning to start a basic police academy for Iraqi police recruits in Amman. About 3 dozen people were needed there to set the academy up and I inquired about joining the team. So I called Alexis and told her – "You aren't going to believe this, but what an opportunity…" (This comment will repeat itself over the next three years). She said go for it and I did. It meant a delay in my return home, but I really wanted more of the international experience.

Shortly after arrival in Jordan, I learned of a similar mission in Iraq. So I inquired about it then called Alexis: "You aren't going to believe this, but…"

The next thing I knew I was in Iraq in the spring of 2004. At first many of us lived in the red zone at The Baghdad Hotel and commuted to the Police Academy. We traveled in groups and drove fast and furious, armed with pistols and assault rifles. The rule was: whoever wasn't driving was prepared to be a defensive shooter. But shortly after our arrival violence markedly increased, making travel too dangerous, so we had to leave the Baghdad Hotel to go live in open bay barracks right at the police academy, still in the red zone. The academy training was then being conducted by the US Military, who lived on the grounds, so we were reasonably safe. Well, except for the few times the Academy got hit by mortars but no contractor was seriously hurt. It was a violent summer and this certainly added to the excitement. I had the opportunity to work with the Iraqi police in developing both recruits and new Iraqi trainers – what an incredible task.

I finally went home that September, after one year abroad, working in three countries. But the adventure was not yet over. A couple months later, my friends and fellow contractors in Iraq called and asked me to come back. I talked to Alexis – "You aren't going to believe this…" I returned to Iraq for three months to help out during a staffing crisis. I returned home again in February 2005.

A couple months later, the same colleagues called again from Iraq and I talked to Alexis – "you aren't going to believe this…" Another tour in Iraq, this time for six months.

I returned home in November of 2005 thinking I might be done with foreign missions. However, once more, a colleague called, this time about Afghanistan. So I talked to Alexis – you get the idea… I went to Afghanistan for a six month tour. That tour was tough for me. I could have stayed longer, but sometimes you simply have to know when it is time to leave. All missions will test you, some will disappoint you, while others will allow you to enjoy the country and the people while you are truly helping them .

Is This For Me?
Do Some Homework:

There are some incredible people in these emerging countries. You will see the best and the worst as you travel to different parts of the world, both in yourself and other people.

I recommend that you do some homework before deciding if foreign missions are for you. These steps should include:

- What conditions are you willing to live and work in? Even the highest paying jobs have a variety of living and working conditions – from tents to the occasional 5 star hotels (don't expect a 5 star hotel). Some people leave because of the primitive conditions even though they were told about them prior to deployment. Sometimes they expected better conditions because friends were in better spots in the same country. Or they just didn't believe how bad it can sometimes be.

- Are you willing to go into a combat zone? You may or may not be armed. You may or may not control your in-country travel methods. You may be assigned to a military unit and be taking direction from them. Fortunately, not all missions are in combat zones.

- Are you willing to be gone for a year or more? Shorter term assignments are few and far in between, but all the companies that I am aware of allow vacations to go home or visit other locations.

- Is your family supportive of all aspects of the mission? If not, are you really prepared to go against their wishes?

- Loss of identity: You will leave behind your regular life and much of what defines who you are. You may find yourself in a stressful and poorly defined environment where you have to improvise, adapt, and overcome. Intolerance of ambiguity and the need for clear structure does not bode well.

- Loss of social support: You will leave behind your family, colleagues, and friends, and you may or may not find other people to bond with. The possible resulting social isolation can be very difficult for some people to cope with. On the other hand, you may meet people who will become friends for life.

- Loneliness affects nearly everyone at some point, especially if there are family crises or milestones you cannot be there for.

- How comfortable are you with language barriers? When I was working as trainer, I had to work through an interpreter. In Kosovo everything had be translated into two local languages with two different interpreters and it took some getting used to. In addition to teamwork with your interpreters, it requires patience and learning how to pace your work to accommodate the extra time and effort required getting your ideas across. Your usual jokes often won't survive the translation.

- How comfortable are you with politics? Yes, politics are a fact of life with every job. However, in a foreign mission you will be less familiar with the players and you will not have the allies you are used to counting on in your present assignment. With players from different agencies and countries the politics may get complicated, so being a quick study of the political landscape can be important. This is especially true in the upper management positions. If you take things personally and hate politics, it's best you stay retired!

- How comfortable are you with different cultures? The things you will find to admire in foreign countries is the easy part. However, you may see levels of overt sexism, racism, religious intolerance, and/or other customs that would not be acceptable in your home country and may be personally offensive. Your ability to emotionally distance yourself and be realistic about what you can accomplish can become important survival skills.

- Food and water: Unlike popular tourist locations with sanitized hotels, you may end up in places where you'll be exposed to food and water that is unfamiliar and unpalatable and, even worse, may not be safe to eat or drink. You need be prepared to cope with these gastronomical challenges.

- Are you willing to live and work for extended periods in third world countries where threat of disease, less adequate health care, conflict, relative lack of law and order, and other stressors and dangers may exist?

- Are you willing to have limited access to telephone, internet, and mail communications? This varies from place to place, but decide how important this is and then determine accessibility before accepting any assignment.

- Health and life insurance coverage for a contractor may be an issue. Check your personal insurer to make sure you are covered if you are out of your native country or in a combat zone. Check with the company who is hiring you to see what they offer.

- As a contractor you will be without the job security and entitlements you are accustomed to as a regular employee. You will serve at the will of the employer and the terms of your contract will often state that you can be terminated at any time. Your specific contract could include lots of qualifiers; my intent is to point out there is often no legal entitlement to a job.

- The pay scale varies so decide what amount you are willing to work for. Some missions are in great locations with sightseeing opportunities or other perks that make up for lower salaries.

- Many missions are an international effort so you may find yourself working with, or for, colleagues from other countries. This has been one of the most interesting aspects of the adventure, getting to meet people from all over the world!

Getting Started

In addition the US, the UN and the European Union also support missions in many countries so there is ample opportunity for overseas work once you get your foot in the door. How do you find these missions?

Let me say up front that I am not affiliated with any company or governmental organization. I have worked for three different companies and a variety of government agencies over the past three years. I am not advocating one route over any other. Your organization or country may already have connections or commitments, so it is worth exploring. There are many companies out there that provide services at any given time. I recommend that you any research private companies that you may want to work for. To help you get started, try simple Internet inquires like: police missions; or police training; or check with your national government to see what is currently offered.

Once you have decided you are interested, you need to decide what you want to do and your qualifications are. Then start your internet search on those specific topic areas. The best advice I can offer you is to search the net for overseas law enforcement opportunities. There are simply too many categories and companies to list here. It is important to remember that once you have proven yourself as a hard working and effective contractor in your first mission, you have a greater chance of being selected for future missions.

If you decide to take the plunge I hope you will find the trials and rewards of foreign mission work as interesting as I have. Maybe I'll see you over there. Be sure to say hi.

Dave Butzer retired as an Assistant Chief from the Portland Police Bureau in Oregon after being on active duty from 1972 to 1999. Chief Butzer's assignments were diverse, including: patrol, crime prevention, precinct commander; community policing assignments, command of the Domestic Violence Unit, command of the Gang Enforcement Team, command of the Fiscal Division, and public information officer assignments.

Chief Butzer has a strong interest and background in training. He started early in his career at the Portland Police Bureau and has continued in this role as a trainer and senior manager of training until the present day. Chief Butzer and his wife, retired police psychologist Dr. Alexis Artwohl (www.alexisartwohl.com), did training seminars together from 1999-2003 in the area of police use of force.

In 2003, Chief Butzer was selected to be part of a training team deployed to Kosovo to deliver community policing training in four cities. While in Kosovo, he was part of a small group of handpicked police professionals to go to Amman, Jordan, to start up the primary training academy for the recruits of the Iraq Police Service. While in Jordan, Chief Butzer was one of four people selected to deploy to Baghdad to implement the USA led, civilian operated, police training programs. He concluded one year overseas and returned home in 2004.

Chief Butzer subsequently returned to Baghdad, Iraq, twice in 2004 and 2005, with his last assignment being the Director of Police Training for the US led Coalition.

In 2006, Chief Butzer served in Afghanistan filling a number of senior management positions inside the USA led Coalition helping with the mission is to "man, train, equip and operationalize" the Afghan Police Service.

In 2007, he was selected as an instructor auditor for the US Department of Homeland Security grant programs.

Assistant Chief David S. Butzer (Retired)
Law Enforcement Training and Consultation
12995 N. Oracle Road, Suite 141-207
Tucson, Arizona USA 85739
Phone: 520-204-6012   Fax: 520-818-2162
E-mail: davebutzer@msn.com

Training Insights

"Destiny is not a matter of chance; it's a matter of choice. It is not a thing to be waited for; it is a thing to be achieved."

- William Jennings Bryan

TRAINING GAPS

by Brian Willis

Law enforcement training has evolved dramatically since I went through basic training in 1979. There are some great training programs within North America that address officer safety issues such as subject control tactics, tactical firearms training, vehicle stops, rapid intervention, and the use of the myriad of less lethal technology available for officers. Within firearms and subject control tactics agencies are doing a better job of moving from away training officers to qualify and instead training them to win fights.

As training advances and programs and technology become more comprehensive one issue that continues to exist is 'Training Gaps'. By Training Gaps I am referring to three primary areas of concern:

1. Missing elements in training.
2. Training that is not reflective of reality.
3. Training that is incomplete.

Missing Elements In Training

When I talk about missing elements in training I am referring to skills or tactics that may be critical in saving an officer's life but have never been covered in any training. These gaps are often a result of:

- An assumption made by trainers in one area of expertise (i.e. control tactics) that the skill or tactics were covered, or is the responsibility of another area of expertise (i.e. firearms) and vice versa.

- An assumption is made that the officer will be able to fill in the blanks and solve new problems in the middle of a violent encounter.

Let me share an example. During my *Excellence in Training* instructor development courses I often show a video clip from the Calibre Press video 'The Ultimate Survivors'. The clip is a re-creation of an event that took place in the mid 1970's in Baton Rouge, Louisiana. During this situation two officers are searching a home where a possible break in has occurred. When they get to the last room of the house they are confronted by a subject who had broken into the home and was hiding in the bedroom. The officers quickly find themselves in a violent confrontation with the subject at the end of which one of the officers is injured and the other officer and the subject are dead. In discussions that follow the video the majority of officers in every class are critical of what they perceive as a lack of action on the part of one of the officers (the officer who has been killed). After much discussion, it becomes clear that what they believe this officer, acting as the cover officer, should have done was to close the distance and make a contact shot to the subject's head while the subject was fighting with the contact officer over the officer's gun. While this is a sound tactic it identifies a training gap since almost no agencies are now training, or have ever trained their recruits and/or patrol officers to close on a threat and either make a contact shot with a revolver or take the shot from an inch away with a pistol. By training I mean that the tactic was discussed as to when and where this would be appropriate and then the officers actually practiced the skill.

During my informal surveys conducted with the hundreds of officers who have taken part in these discussions I have had two that indicated their agency conducted this type of training for their officers as part of recruit training in the 1970's. Only a handful of officers indicate that their agency trained this in the 1980's and 1990's and it appears very few agencies are including this as part of their recruit training in the 21st century. Some officers did indicate that it was part of SWAT training. This is not good enough. We must train it at the recruit and in-service level. If agencies are not training officers to use this tactic is it reasonable to expect that in the heat of battle, during a close and violent fight for their lives that an officer will miraculously come up with this tactic in order to save their life? The answer is no. Therefore, a training gap exists.

The aspect of winning close, violent encounters in which officers are confronted by an attacker committed to killing him or her is one where a number of training gaps exist. These encounters take many forms including edged weapons attacks, officer hostage situations, disarming attempts and gunfights and often occur in the confines of narrow hallways, stairwells, small rooms and other close quarter environments. It is critical for the officer who finds him or herself in this situation to be trained and conditioned to use overwhelming violence to defeat the attacker and win the confrontation.

For the officer this overwhelming violence may mean:

- Driving his or her fingers into the subject's eyes to permanently or temporarily take away the subject's ability to see and in the process the willingness and ability to fight;
- Striking the subject's throat with a forearm, elbow or fisted strike to affect his or her ability to breathe - again influencing the willingness and ability to continue the attack;
- Striking the attacker in the head or neck with a baton, flashlight or radio;
- Accessing a folding knife, which the officer carries as a general purpose utility tool or rescue tool, and stabbing or slashing the attacker to end the confrontation;
- Using a pen, rock, brick, bottle, or 2 x 4 as a weapon of opportunity;
- Placing the officer's handgun within inches of the subject's head, or torso and firing rounds into the subject until he or she ceases being a threat.

If we can accept that ferocity of action and overwhelming violence are *What's Important Now* for the officer to win the confrontation and allow him or her to go home to family, then we must ask ourselves if our training programs mentally and physically prepare officers to accomplish this? Too often the honest answer is NO. There are still too many programs where this critical element of training is missing from both in-service and academy use of force training. In many agencies the closest an officer ever gets to a target that he or she will shoot, or simulate shooting, with a handgun is 7 feet. Head shots are often only executed at distance and either on command or as part of a pre-determined course of fire (i.e. when the target turns you will fire two rounds to the body and one to the head.). In too many agencies officers never get the opportunity to practice striking a violent attacker in the throat or attacking their eyes. They are never told that it is OK to use weapons of opportunity such as a pen, knife, brick, radio, or a flashlight in these situations to strike a subject in the head, throat or spine. Because it is not part of training too many officers have never truly imagined being in a close and violent fight for their life. Therefore, there are no programs or files in the subconscious mind that the officer can fall back on in these tense, violent and rapidly evolving situations and in too many cases the outcome for the officer is less desirable.

Excuses

Time, safety and political sensitivity are common excuses or justifications that we as trainers come up with for not conducting this training. These excuses are ALL unacceptable. These training gaps get officers killed and injured and must be addressed. Simple drills can be easily and safely built into existing training time within control tactics, weapon retention, defeating edged weapons attacks, weapon disarming (officer hostage), and/or building clearing.

Safety in training must always be the paramount consideration. This issue however, is simple to address. Start slow and build on the principles and concepts during the training program. When training officers to make in-close head or body shots the officers can safely train with peers acting as the subject by utilizing plastic training guns (it is important to make sure the officer goes through the motions of pulling the trigger). The officers can then progress to using training dummies or photo realistic targets using weapons configured for non-lethal training ammunition (NLTA). Striking dummies can also be used to teach attacks to the throat and eyes and create the opportunity for officers to strike these areas with power. By cutting out the eyes on the training dummies and replacing them with fake ones the officers can get the feel of actually driving their fingers into a subject's eye sockets. When training with other officers they can train themselves to make light contact to the eyes while imagining driving their fingers deep into the subject's eye sockets. Swim goggles or other protective eyewear can be worn by those playing the role of the subjects to help protect their eyes during this training.

Finally, we cannot allow perceived political sensitivity to stand in the way of potentially life saving training. This training is not designed to turn officers into brutish thugs who go around and poke out peoples eyes and crush their throats for the sport of it. It is designed to teach officers what they can do to save their lives when they find themselves the subject of a violent attack. During these types of encounters it is easily articulated that these tactics fall within the parameters of actions that are both reasonable and necessary based on the totality of circumstances.

The key for all of us is to stop making excuses and start doing this critical training. Excuses get officers hurt and killed; realistic training saves lives.

Training That is Not Reflective of Realty

By now, all officers and trainers should have accepted the reality that no tool or technique is 100% effective, 100% of the time on 100% of the subjects that are confronted. Subjects can and have defeated OC spray, conducted energy weapons (CEW), baton strikes, kicks and gunshot wounds. Once we acknowledge this reality the critical question to ask is: do the current training programs prepare officers for when these tools and techniques fail? Too often the answer is no. In fact, in many cases the training convinces officers that these force options will always work in the field. I believe this occurs for three main reasons:

1. In an effort to convince officers of the value of a tool or technique and make them confident trainers give the impression that the tool will always work.
2. In the interests of time and in the name of liability, agencies have simply adopted the manufacturers training protocols. Manufacturers training programs are generally designed to sell their product by convincing officers how effective their particular tool is. They often fail to address the totality of use of force and in some circumstances do not teach officers what to do when the tool fails. And it will fail.
3. In some agencies use of force training is still fragmented and different trainers teach the different force options with little or no tie in between sessions. Even if one training cadre teaches all the subject control tactics and less lethal technology, they are rarely the same people who deliver firearms training.

All three of these situations are breeding grounds for training gaps and regardless of how or why it happened, steps must be taken to correct this oversight. Officers, in training, must be exposed to drills where their OC, their CEW, their batons strikes, their kicks and punches, and their initial shots fail to stop the threat. When the tool or techniques fails the officer must be taught how to transition to an alternate target area on the subject's body, or to transition to a different force response option in order to defeat the threat and gain control of the subject. These failure drills are a simple, but often overlooked element of training.

Incomplete Training

There are times in training where we fail to provide a complete experience for officers. An example is when a reality based training scenario is stopped as soon as the subject gets shot. In reality, the situation is far from over at the point where the subject is shot. What's Important Now are such critical issues as:

- Is the threat actually stopped?
- Is the officer in the most desirable tactical position?
- Does anyone else know where the officer is and what has happened?
- Is the officer injured?
- Are there other threats the officer needs to address?

If the training does not incorporate these and other issues into it by having the officer address and complete those tasks then the training is incomplete and a training gap exists. The result may be less desirable as the officer may momentarily freeze and fail to address these critical issues. In order to engrain this response into the subconscious officers must be trained in these tactics. In order for them to be trained the scenarios must be played out to their conclusion. At the very least these areas must be addressed in the debriefing so that the officer at least has the opportunity to imagine the full scenario and create the files in his subconscious.

The same gap also occurs when officers are trained using video interactive judgmental use of force simulators (FATS, PRISM, etc). When the scenario ends and the screen goes blank, too often the training simply stops and the debriefing begins. Again, this is incomplete training and therefore a training gap exists. A more desirable way to complete this training would be to utilize other officers as role players and have them continue with the scenario from the various positions that people were in when the screen went blank. This will force the officer involved in the scenario to assess the threat(s), assess his or her tactical position, call for assistance on the radio and determine the next course of action. By adding this simple step the mental loop for the officer is completed and he or she is better prepared for the realities in the field.

The challenge to every single officer and trainer is to continue to ask What's Important Now (W.I.N.)? What is important is that we set aside our egos, take a step back, and examine how we train our brother and sister law enforcement professionals and ourselves. As part of this self-examination process it is important to ask ourselves:

- Does our training reflect reality?
- Are we truly training officers to win, or inadvertently setting them up to fail?
- Do we train with imagination and emotion, or do we go through the motions in training?
- What gaps exist in our training?
- What steps do we need to take to eliminate those gaps?

W.I.N. – three simple letters with a powerful message for all of us.

Brian Willis is an internationally recognized trainer and speaker. Brian draws on his 25 years of law enforcement experience as a member of the Calgary Police Service and over 19 years of training experience to provide cutting edge training to law enforcement officers and trainers throughout North America. Brian has been honored with a Lifetime Achievement Award in recognition of his contributions to officer safety training in Canada.

Brian operates Winning Mind Training and Warrior Spirit Books (www.warriorspiritbooks.com) and is the editor of the highly acclaimed books W.I.N.: Critical Issues in Training and Leading Warriors as well as a contributing writer for the book Warriors: On Living With Courage, Discipline and Honor (www.warriorspiritbooks.com).

Brian serves as an Advisory Board member for the International Law Enforcement Educators and Trainers Association (ILEETA), and served as a member of the National Advisory Board for Police Marksman Magazine from 2000 to 2007. He is a member of NTOA, ITOA, IALEFI, National Guild of Hypnotists and the Canadian

Association of Professional Speakers. He is the Editor of the ILEETA Review and writes a regular column for the ILEETA Use of Force Journal. Brian can be reached through his website at www.winningmindtraining.com.

DEGREES OF POLICE TRAINING

by Mike Starchuk

*"Consistency is the last refuge
of the unimaginative."*

- Oscar Wilde

At one time or another, in all locations and fields of study, conscientious trainers eventually ask themselves, what is it that I really need to teach these people? When that has been answered, two follow up questions must be resolved: to what degree and what is the best method for accomplishing the task at hand? Narrowing the scope of the questions to the field of law enforcement actually broadens the answer to the first question in that people must be trained to be safe: operationally, procedurally, legally, mentally and from civil jurisprudence. Certainly it is true that training law enforcement personnel has been on going for sometime and if the basic fundamentals of dealing with people haven't changed that much why raise these issues now? The short answer is that changes brought about through technology and the information age demands a re-examination of our training paradigms.

To begin this discussion let me state that this is a great time to be involved in law enforcement training! I have worked with and continue to work with intelligent, highly skilled, and very dedicated officers who truly want to ensure that training programs make people safer. It is a deliberate choice to describe the end goal of increasing safety for people as: if officers receive proper training, everyone benefits including the citizens they are charged with protecting. Current technology provides any trainer with instantaneous access to research, historical and breaking news events, data, documentation, programs, incident analysis, and situational videos to name only a few potential and valuable training tools. With this sheer volume of material, decisions need to be made as to the relevancy, how much and when the information harvested through technology needs to be included into a training program. Improvements to programs can be made to take advantage of the latest thinking in tactics, techniques, mental preparedness.

At the entry level, most basic academy courses are limited by resources including the need to efficiently deliver the material in a cost effective and timely manner. Subject matter trainers staying abreast of the latest developments will undoubtedly come across new methodologies that are both relevant and necessary for future officers to have and experience. The problem facing them is how to incorporate the new material into the current model. The answer does not lie in simply extending the training program or adding more home study nor can it be resolved by cutting material that may be part of mandated standards or a POST curriculum. The solution to this situation involves formally shifting training well beyond the academy doors.

The vast majority of law enforcement agencies provide pay incentives that correspond with steps, grades, and time spent as a police officer. These are designed with the belief that experience and knowledge acquired through doing the job has value. Another way to look at this is that it takes time to develop the education, skills, proficiencies, and abilities to be an effective police officer. The first few years of patrol work is similar to a trade apprenticeship program or maybe the better way to look at is to compare it to an undergraduate program at a college or university. In this comparison, a three or four year degree would be comparable to a first class constable, patrol officer three or for a rookie to reach a first grade position. The time spent earning a college degree involves academic studies along with work experience until the requisites have been achieved and the student graduates. It can be argued that once the degree has been obtained, it is truly the starting point for the individual to begin working in his or her chosen field of study. This is true for law enforcement as well.

The paradigm shift is to acknowledge that the basic academy course is similar to the first year of college and that additional training is required to move officers toward their "degree." Academy classes need to form the base so that the officers are safe and competent as a first year officer. For example in a number of academies, new officers are provided information and learn tactics to check or clear a premise where a break in has occurred, an alarm has been activated or following a firearm complaint once all the know threats have been removed from the crisis point. This training ranges from classroom discussion to table top exercises to complex scenarios involving trained role players and non lethal training ammunition and weaponry. However, once the officer has left the academy, are we confident that these perishable skills they once learned are being used? Additionally, is any experiential learning further enhancing the officers' skill set or in the alternative are short cuts being taken in favor of expediency or a lack of resources? Are we prepared to accept that the lack of an officer safety incident is the measure of the success of basic training?

An argument can be made that unlike university programs, law enforcement requires that newly graduated officers spend additional time training with an experienced field trainer to provide guidance, mentorship, and evaluation as to how the student officer applies their skills in the real world. Even though field training is an integral part of development, the experience gained will be different for each individual as their geographic patrol assignment, work style of their trainer and even luck of the draw in relation to their call load will determine their experience on the street. To address this issue, any knowledge or skill gaps can be filled through planned and formalized second year training that builds upon the base level of knowledge. This also allows for officers to receive the latest information relating to tactics, techniques and legal theory which the academy may not have had time to fully address or develop. In this model, training has a contextual base as officers have their own point of reference from which to fuel increased learning.

This is certainly not to say that the second year training needs to mirror the academy in length nor in subject matter but it needs to be relevant to identified competencies that would be expected of a second year officer. With some street time under the belt, it would be expected that training related to search warrant applications would be better suited for a second or even third year officer as opposed to the basic academy. At issue here is not the fact that an agency can provide in-service training, but rather a decisive recognition that the journey from a recruit to four year officer demands a planned series of progressive training with each block building upon the previous levels. We can not do it all in the basic academy so the challenge is to determine the essential core material from the perspective that the officers will receive further training at a future fixed interval.

Since the doorway to the comparison of law enforcement training to college programs has been opened, it can also serve as a foundation for addressing people who fail to meet the standard of a basic core competency. If a person fails to achieve a grade point standard in an undergraduate college course they are not necessarily expunged from the faculty but rather they can retake the course of instruction at their own expense. For the most part they will need the course to fulfill their degree requirement just as the police officer requires successful completion of the basics in order to be safe. However, unlike the college, police officers undergo a comprehensive selection process in order to gain access to the academy with the goal being to identify desirable candidates for the profession. Should an officer be deficient in one area, it is reasonable that they be afforded the opportunity to continue training but the deficient area training should be at their expense. After all, since they were of value to enter the academy why not continue to work with them until they succeed or self-deselect?

Let me cite an example related to pursuit driving and tactics which are essential skills for officers to possess. Is it critical for officers to have that training before they move onto the field training phase? If there is no follow up training then clearly the answer is yes but how effective is that academy training? If an officer had time in a patrol vehicle, was familiar with the vehicle equipment including the lap top, radio usage and protocols a case could be made that this initial training would be more effective and efficient by reducing the slope of the learning curve as the officer now possesses some of the key sub-skills required for effective pursuit driving. This is not to suggest that the pursuit training be shifted to the second year of training but rather at some point during field training - four, eight, or twelve weeks beyond the academy in order to provide an opportunity for increased learning. While in the field training phase, the new officers would be prohibited from driving in pursuit mode until completion of their respective training. It is important to remember that pursuit driving is a higher order skill set and this serves to illustrate the point that it may be time to shift perspective on law enforcement training. Critical examination of the basic curriculum will certainly reveal other topics or subjects that may be better suited for training beyond the academy.

I am sure that everyone has heard veteran officers describe the current job as a lot more complicated than it use to be. Law enforcement is becoming more complex not only for the knowledge required for officers to be safe but at a pace that hasn't been seen before. As demands and expectations for superior police performance continue to be echoed from the public, media and all levels of government officials it is imperative that trainers continue with their dedicated efforts to train law enforcement officers to be safe. The end point of this essay is really a challenge for trainers as that is truly where the catalyst for change will occur: are you prepared to fundamentally and formally shift training beyond the academy doors and to what degree?

Mike Starchuk is a law enforcement trainer whose career has spanned over 30 years in a large metropolitan police service. He has spent over 14 years as a full time trainer primarily dedicated to emergency vehicle operations, officer safety tactics, and strategic communications. He has been directly involved in training over a thousand law enforcement officers ranging from recruit level to experienced officers. Additionally he has developed and taught instructor level training programs. Although he has retired from his sworn officer position, he has remained on full time staff as a consultant and physical skills instructor. He can be contacted at mikestarchuk@mac.com.

PLAN TO TRAIN, OR PLAN TO FAIL

by Steven D. Ashley

Quality in-service training is what allows most police officers to function safely and effectively. In short, training provides an opportunity for a department to grow and excel. It goes without saying that anything that will safely enhance effectiveness is a resource to be nurtured and exploited. Yet the law enforcement profession continues to lose training opportunities on an almost daily basis.

The training function has been routinely relegated to a secondary role in many police agencies. The daily press of more urgent matters tends to gobble resources and squander work hours until very little of anything is left to fulfill the need for training and human resource development.

Of course, police officers are employed to protect lives and property, not to sit in class—both the public and government officials (and therefore the Chief or Sheriff) see more cops on the street as the answer to society's security problems. When push comes to shove, resources have to be allocated to covering patrol shifts and doing follow-up investigations, because police are expected to prevent and/or solve as much crime as possible in order to keep society and its citizens safe.

Historically, this has been the public's primary expectation regarding their police agencies, and, by and large, law enforcement officers have risen to the challenge. But those expectations are changing, and professional law enforcement has to begin changing as well.

The Costs of Crisis

While we may be holding the line on crime (an issue which many would choose to debate), we are losing the battle of the budget. We are spending huge amounts of both money and goodwill as a result of incidents involving alleged excessive force, improper motor vehicle operation and false arrest. It has been estimated that forty cents of every liability dollar paid out by communities goes to cover jury awards, settlements and legal fees related to police claims. Forty percent! And these are only the direct, liability related costs.

How does one calculate the value of eroded public confidence in law enforcement? When we make a big splash in the media through some inappropriate act or ill-conceived policy, the ripples are felt for years. Over time, reduced public confidence in and respect for the law enforcement profession leads to tighter budgets, reductions in resources, and unemployed Chiefs and Sheriffs. Our partnership with the community breaks down, and the crooks very ably take advantage of a bad situation.

Perhaps most importantly, our police officers and deputies suffer. They are subjected to ridicule and suspicion on the street, and in the press. This negative environment cannot help but have a significant impact on morale, and therefore performance. Over time, increased job-related stress can lead to serious chronic health problems, excessive sick leave, and early retirements, thus robbing us of our most experienced people.

Officers are frequently injured in motor vehicle and use of force incidents. Worker's compensation insurers report that the most common situation leading to officer injury is a resisted arrest. Additionally, many officers are injured annually as a result of motor vehicle accidents.

So, what can we do about it? We can start fighting the right battle. We can recognize that well trained, disciplined officers will cost us less in the long run than partially trained, directionless ones. **We can realign our priorities, with training at the very top of the list.**

Planning Change

We must get ahead of the curve, and reduce our tendency to think reactively. We must be strategic thinkers rather than crisis managers. The answer lies in strategic management of the training process and the pragmatic application of a training plan.

When a department outlines its approach to training management, five key aspects should be included:

- People - Delegation & involvement
- Information - Collection & analysis
- Policy Development
- Strategic Planning
- Program Maintenance

These key program aspects, and all of their incorporated elements, interact to form a training management system that will allow a Chief or Sheriff to think strategically while allocating resources to training.

People Power - Delegate, Don't Dictate

One reason that police managers frequently find themselves shifting into "crisis management mode" is their tendency to try to do too much. The majority of police agencies in the United States have fewer than fifteen officers. In this environment, the Chief spends a great deal of time patrolling and answering calls, as well as managing daily business. There simply isn't time to devote to research and development of a training program.

Responsibility for the training program should be delegated to a designated training officer. With the limited opportunities for advancement in a small agency, most departments have at least one officer interested in assuming these duties. Ideally, the training assignment would be a full time job, but this will not normally be possible. Generally, the training officer will continue to perform other routine duties.

Another problem that frequently manifests itself where training is concerned is resistance from the ranks. Even the best training program can falter if officers are disinterested or hostile. One useful method for dealing with this possibility is the formation of a training committee, charged with the responsibility for development of new training ideas and plans. Union representatives and supervisory personnel should be invited to join this committee, as support from these individuals can greatly enhance acceptance of the training program. The rank and file of the department will feel some ownership of the training program

Information - From Here to There

When getting directions to any destination, you have to know where you are to begin with. Many departments attempt to make decisions regarding training with little or no information.

There are at least three critical types of information that the police manager needs in order to plan for the best utilization of training resources:
- Any existing training records
- Officer injury and liability loss data
- Available training opportunities

TRAINING RECORDS - The first order of business for any department is to gather all existing training records. While some agencies have kept good records, many have not. Officers should be queried regarding any training records they have that the department does not have. Ideally, a computer database should be constructed, using a relational database program. This will enable the easiest and most efficient management of the information once it is collected.

Remember to collect information on all of each officer's training. Include any training that he or she completed before they joined your department. Emphasize specialized training, such as instructor certifications and supervisory/management training. Consider expanding your training records to include college degrees and other professional certifications, and remember to include specialized military training.

LOSSES and INCIDENTS - In order for training to be truly useful to both the individual officer and to the department, it must be job-related and relevant. An informal review of past incidents will reveal elements of daily operations that have a high potential for officer injury and/or civil liability. These areas should receive a proportionate amount of training resources. Generally, the three areas where police agencies suffer the greatest number of and most costly losses are use of force, operation of motor vehicles, and false arrest.

Remember to track those incidents that don't result in a loss; i.e. successful pursuits, arrests completed without injury, etc. While these incidents didn't lead to injuries or lawsuits, they do indicate activity levels, and such information is critically important to any department's risk management effort.

COURSE OFFERINGS - Because so many agencies are located some distance from training facilities, the police manager must review course offerings several months in advance. This will enable the selection of less costly or more geographically suitable options when selecting training sessions. When a department fails to anticipate its training needs, it is likely to spend more than necessary in travel and accommodation expense, as well as overtime.

In-house training is frequently the most cost-effective strategy for courses that must be taken by all officers on a regular basis, such as defensive tactics or precision driving. This type of training usually requires instructor training and recertification, however, and instructor courses tend to be longer and more infrequently offered. Advance planning is a must when securing instructor training.

Policy Development - Setting Standards

A department's training policy is arguably the most important document in its policy manual. It is through the functional implementation of the training policy that all other aspects of the department's critical operations are controlled.

While each department's policy will differ, there are three essential elements that should be incorporated into all training policies:

TRAINING PHILOSOPHY - The training policy should begin with a statement of the department's position on such issues as professionalism through training, career development and personal growth. This philosophy statement will form the rational basis for the entire program, so it should be thoughtfully developed and carefully written.

ESTABLISHMENT OF STANDARDS - In the process of administering the program, the police manager will encounter situations where fair and equitable standards are needed. These standards can be developed for such areas as instructor selection, pass/fail criteria, remedial training, FTO program completion, recertification in skill areas, and many others.

The training policy should delineate the process by which these various standards will be developed and maintained.

PROGRAM EMPOWERMENT - The training policy will serve as "enabling legislation" for the daily operation of the training program. Such issues as mandatory class attendance, disciplinary procedures and instructor authority should be addressed.

The Plan - Thinking Strategically

The written training plan serves as the program's roadmap, guiding the police manager's allocation of resources toward realization of the department's goals. Everything that we have discussed so far has been geared to one objective – the functional implementation of this written plan.

Development of the plan should begin with the formulation of specific objectives. The police manager will identify the areas of training deemed essential and consistent with the long term goal of safe enhancement of effectiveness.

Once these objectives are defined, training needs should be prioritized. Many factors impact on the priority order of training, and many other training needs will be perceived at this point. The police manager should make every effort to remain focused on the established objectives, especially if resources are scarce.

Lastly, the plan should include a timetable for implementation. The overwhelming shortage of training in many departments (due to department size, limited budgets, or poor training history) indicates a need to plan strategically over a three to five year period. In this manner, portions of the workforce can be platooned annually, lessening the financial burden somewhat.

A final note on planning: Once the plan is developed and implemented, it's likely that situations will arise that necessitate occasional deviations. These should be resisted if possible, and documented when they must occur. An attachment to the plan (in memo form) should indicate the reason for the deviation. In this way, the integrity of the plan can be maintained, and its usefulness as evidence of good faith retained.

Maintenance - Avoiding "GIGO"

Ongoing maintenance of the training program should focus on three central activities: evaluation of classes attended, documentation of training attended, and the periodic adjustment or revision of the training plan.

CLASS EVALUATIONS - Because officers attend classes at different locations, it's not possible for the training officer or police manager to personally attend each session for the purpose of evaluating training content, appropriateness or scope. The department should utilize an evaluation form, to be completed by class attendees and returned to the training officer. This will give officers an opportunity to make their feelings known to the department's administration, and will provide a means of checking on the thoroughness and appropriateness of both program content and style. One method of implementation that many departments use successfully is to provide a combination notice of training assignment and evaluation form.

TRAINING RECORDS - Once the department's training database is constructed, it should be maintained in as complete and timely a manner as possible. The database should at least include the following:

- Training title
- Training dates
- Number of training hours
- Training location
- Training vendor (if different)

PLAN REVISION - Any long-range plan will have to be modified from time to time, based on pressing demands or on new concerns (e.g. the recent push for homeland security training). As time passes, it will be tempting to deviate farther from the original course laid out in the plan.

It is vitally important that deviations from the original plan be valid, job related, and relevant – and that they be documented. Without this control, the usefulness of the training plan as a management tool and as an evidentiary document becomes highly questionable.

While no plan can be cast in stone, all members of the department should understand the necessity for careful planning accompanied by a commitment to avoid deviation.

Of course, any revisions made should be reviewed by the department's training committee, and by senior management.

The Challenge

Having come full circle in our systems approach to training management, it's time to make a commitment. If we are truly serious about improving the relationship between ourselves and the communities that we serve, and if we really do want to enhance professionalism, then we must act now.

We have an absolute obligation to make every reasonable effort to reduce the number of officer and citizen injuries that result from our activities. As police managers and trainers, the responsibility to think strategically so as to best utilize limited resources falls to no one else.

We can't "make" officers be safe and less liability prone, they must decide to do that on their own. We can, however, manage our training resources and efforts in such a way as to provide them with the information they need, in a positive, reinforcing manner. Most officers will respond favorably to such training, and will identify the personal benefit to be gained by professional application of training information. Those who do not can be dealt with through the agency's normal disciplinary process, with less strife and frustration – due to labor's participation in the management of the training process.

Although implementing a well-rounded training management system from scratch can be time consuming, the initial work is well worth the effort, as ongoing maintenance of the program will be much simpler. When a training management program has been fully implemented, many other administrative tasks are more easily handled, with corresponding savings in time and resources.

Today's police managers and trainers are charged with tremendous responsibility. The safety of society and the financial and professional wellbeing of officers and other employees can be a heavy burden, especially when viewed from the perspective of daily crisis management.

Those managers and trainers that are able to think strategically can lighten their load and, at the same time, create a smoother running, safer, more efficient department, with less liability exposure, increased community support, and enhanced officer morale.

Steve Ashley is a retired police officer and a professional risk manager, with over 20 years experience as a police trainer. A much sought after speaker and author, Steve specializes in use of force, vehicle operations, and other areas of high risk law enforcement operations. Email Steve at steve@sashley.com or steveashley@ileeta.org.

TRAINING OFFICERS IN THE REASONABLE EMPLOYMENT OF THE KNIFE

by George T. Williams

Knife carry by US police officers is nearly universal. Almost all carry one knife. Some carry up to four, and one officer reported carrying five while on-duty—all day, all night, every shift. Knives are needed by officers for the normal, mundane tasks for which knives are useful: cutting errant threads, evidence collection, opening boxes and packages, etc. Cops, by the very nature of their job, have additional duties that sometimes require the cutting tasks that only knives can satisfy: rescuing trapped accident victims from vehicles by cutting seatbelts, and freeing persons and animals from (either intentional or accidental) ligature. Another important component that has not been universally acknowledged by police administrators, is the fact that their officers are carrying duty knives as a last-ditch means of defense when there is nothing else that will save them.

A number of police officers have employed their duty knives as a means of surviving desperate assaults. Many officers credit their use of their duty knife with their being alive today. Just a few incidents are:

- 1986: A young officer is losing his handgun to a mentally ill suspect who is under the influence of narcotics and severely outweighs the officer. The officer, being completely overwhelmed, pulls an unauthorized fixed-blade knife he carries in the small of his back and stabs the suspect 28 times and slashes this determined suspect's throat before the officer can once again control his handgun.

- 1999: An officer, who had been knocked unconscious awakens to find himself being pummeled in the face and head by his own flashlight. He fights to his feet only to see his own handgun being shoved at him. The officer grabs the handgun just as the suspect fires three rounds, narrowly missing the officer's face. Knowing that his luck won't hold, the officer produces a folding knife, and swings at the suspect's throat, ending the deadly threat to his life.

- 2006: A deputy is fighting two brothers who each desperately want to stay out of jail. Each is over 300 pounds. One is attempting to take the deputy's handgun, while the other is attempting to remove the deputy's radio. The deputy draws a popular fixed blade knife marketed to police and slashes at the first suspect, who inadvertently slaps the knife out of the deputy's hand (a retention problem with this particular knife design in these situations). The deputy then produces a large folding knife, causing both suspects to stop their assault, and comply with being taken into custody with no further resistance.

These incidents (of which there are many) represent law enforcement's reality: officers carry knives as a last-ditch weapon that may be needed to save their lives. Like it or not, one of your officers may use a knife in a desperate bid to survive a vicious attack on a holstered handgun. To deal with this reality, an agency needs to consider publishing a policy on duty knives, as well as then training their officers in the reasonable, defensible, and limited deadly force response with a knife.

Policy

There is a reasonable reluctance in avoiding having a policy delineating every move an officer makes (who needs a policy delineating the number and type of pens an officer carries?). However, a "duty knife" policy is a needed component for any policy's General Order manual. After all, most police chief executives will testify that they consider the knife carried by their officers to simply be a "tool" used for myriad utility purposes, and was never intended to be employed as a "weapon."

This is a true statement from an administrator's point of view. However, it does not recognize that, when faced with the very real choice of dying or resorting to a knife as a deadly force response, officers will resort to the knife as a deadly weapon. When that knife is employed as a deadly weapon, the "only a tool" theory does not reflect the stark reality of that officer's knife, held in evidence for the last three years, with the suspect-now-decedent's dried blood on the blade, being displayed to the jury in court.

The plaintiff's attorney will mockingly state that while the defendant police administrators are attempting to portray this object as a "tool," they are simply trying to avoid responsibility for permitting their officers to carry and use a "deadly weapon" without policy guidance or training. It will be declared, and plaintiffs will attempt to convince the jury that this lack of policy and training directly led to the violations resulting in the decedent's demise.

While carried and used for utility purposes 99.9% of the time by officers, the knife, having been employed in a deadly force response, will be seen as a deadly weapon by the media, citizens, and juries. The jury will be told over and over, and will likely believe, that the officer's administration knew (or should have known) that his or her defendant officer was carrying a deadly weapon. It will be pointed out that the administration chose not to regulate the knife's carry or use by policy and training. And it will be forcefully argued that, with reckless disregard and deliberate indifference resulting in the decedent's death, it was the failure to control and direct their officers possession and use of the knife that was the cause in fact of the loss of life.

Policy Components. Duty knife policy components can include any desired limitations on size (e.g., blade length less than five inches), style (e.g., no tanto shaped blades), mechanisms (e.g., automatics are permitted or not; fixed blades are permitted only when concealed, etc.), and the number of knives permitted to be carried (if that is seen as important by administration). Additionally, there should be a policy language requiring the responsible and safe use of the knife as a utility tool.

The last policy component to consider is regarding the use of the knife as a weapon. Some police administrators have gone so far as to issue policies with mandatory language stating that knives are utility tools for cutting purposes only, and "shall not be employed as a weapon."

This is a solution that will be doomed to either failure or tragedy. The result will be that an officer, under threat to his or her life, will either deliberately disregard policy in order to survive (very understandable), while another officer, more afraid of losing his or her job than the reality of being murdered, will not, and will be killed after losing the handgun. This ill-considered provision will likely result in either a justified homicide that is simultaneously a flagrant policy violation (resulting in a difficult to defend state tort lawsuit), or the officer's murder and another police funeral.

Instead, the policy should recognize that while not intended as a "primary" deadly force weapon, this tool is permitted to be employed as a last-ditch option to save a person's life. Just as any good force policy permits the officer to employ any means or implement that is reasonable to the context of the situation, so should it permit the reasonable response with the knife as a deadly force option.

Training

Once policy is established, the next step in protecting both the agency and the officers from unwanted liability exposure is through implementing training to support the policy, with the express purpose of creating a "trained" response by officers. This training needs to support the objective reasonableness standard required by Scott v. Harris (2007) and Graham v. Conner (1989). Additionally, the training should support a philosophy of the limited employment of the knife. The limited employment of the knife attempts to decrease the perception of misconduct by lessening the number of wounds inflicted while balancing the need to be effective at stopping a deadly assault quickly enough to effectively factor into the officer's survival.

Avoiding Primitive Conduct. This training must always account for the very real requirement of justifying the officer's actions years after the event where a jury might have a limited understanding of the viciousness and determination of the suspect in creating an imminent deadly threat. Through training, the likelihood of an officer resorting to the "primitive conduct" seen in the incident in 1988, as related earlier in this article, is significantly lessened.

Primitive conduct results without a trained understanding in the effective employment of the knife as a deadly force response tool. An officer, in a desperate measure to prevent his losing his handgun, hits the suspect and then withdraws the knife. There is now a problem. Unless the suspect understands (and is capable of registering) that there is a knife in the officer's hand and he has been stabbed, there will likely be no change in behavior because of the nature of knife wounds.

Knives do not shock the system like bullets hitting a body does, and often times a knife wound is not discovered for minutes, or even hours post-event. Even after being hit with a simple, but possibly fatal knife wound, the weapon retention assault will often continue unless the suspect consciously chooses to stop. The officer, observing no change in the threat to his life, hits the suspect again. And again. And again. And again, until the suspect either chooses to desist and comply, or loses sufficient total blood volume so as to be rendered unconscious.

There is no inherent "unreasonableness" to any number of knife strikes as a deadly force response needed to stop an assaultive subject, just as there is no intrinsic issue with a large number of rounds hitting a suspect in any shooting, as long as the totality of the facts support these wounds. However, multiple knife wounds, like multiple gunshot wounds, complicate the justification of the officer's actions to the uneducated, both within policing and in the public—what was your reaction to the first account of the young officer saving his life by resorting to 28 knife wounds and a slash to the throat? The public's perception, as well as that of some police administrators', that "more" is somehow wrong will also be a factor in any post-deadly force response justification—again suggesting the need for a training philosophy of limited employment of the knife.

Competent, *police-oriented* deadly force training helps restrain primitive behavior, even when the officer is on the brink of being murdered. This training incorporates an employment philosophy that requires each officer to justify via law and policy *during training* the reason and manner in which that officer responded with deadly force. It provides a balance of effective employment of the knife with restraint and defensible conduct, understanding that there are two parts to any force response: overcoming offender resistance AND justifying the reasonableness of the response, based on the officer's understanding of the totality of the circumstances known at the time, through reporting, documentation, and integrous testimony.

Problematic training philosophies. If all officers who carry the knife need training, in what system and how should they be trained? Many agency trainers wrongly fall back upon traditional knife "martial arts" as the basis of training officers. Filipino and Indonesian knife fighting are the primary method for these trainers...after all, they are the best at "knife fighting," aren't they?

While one could argue for or against that statement depending upon one's informed or uninformed position, it is wholly irrelevant to the subject of training police officers to safely, effectively, and reasonably employ the knife. **POLICE OFFICERS DON'T KNIFE FIGHT, AND SHOULD NOT BE TRAINED IN KNIFE FIGHTING.** Law enforcement officers respond with deadly force, and are lawfully permitted to employ any tool as a weapon in a deadly force response in a very limited circumstance. The police will never, ever fight "knife-on-knife" with a suspect. Therefore, all "knife-on-knife" training drills are inappropriate for police. All training teaching incorporating the maximum infliction of damage through the use of a knife via "flow drills" against another person, with the non-officer partner "defending" against the officer's multiple "attacks," as well as teaching officers to employ "trapping, checking, and numbered strikes," is inherently and fundamentally flawed for police. Any of this training that is not situation specific and immediately relevant to an officer's reasonable conduct and survival should be immediately eliminated from consideration as training.

Additionally, all training must be within the confines and limits of law enforcement's time limitations in teaching defense and control skills. At least 85% of law enforcement has no more than 100 hours of defensive tactics training in their lives, much less during their careers. A non-derogatory term for these officers is the "85%er," describing the lowest 85% of police officers in terms of capabilities, physical fitness and strength, and motivation—not everyone is an Olympic athlete, and even among the Olympic Team, there are 85%ers. As such, ALL defensive tactics training must be geared toward making the 85%er successful when facing a determined, prepared offender.

Anyone seeking to teach the average officer (the 85%'er) how to "fight" with a knife in the Kali or Escrima-style is, frankly, wasting everyone's time. It is too complicated, won't be practiced, and, more importantly, is completely irrelevant to how the officer will reasonably employ the knife. Officers need training to meet specific, limited on-duty life-and-death circumstances where the knife is a 100% viable option and, vitally, a reasonable deadly force response. Additionally, training must be durable. That is, very complicated techniques requiring fine timing and skill will be extremely perishable, and will likely be forgotten by the time the officer leaves the training floor. An officer must have durable training that will be easy to recall, practical to employ, and capable of success in the most dire of extremes.

All martial arts "knife" training, as well as any "military-based" program, is inherently inappropriate for law enforcement application. Before becoming stylized, most martial arts began as a military solution to a battlefield problem. On the battlefield, the use of an edged metal weapons was, and remains solely employed to kill an opposing enemy soldier. The goal in the employment of the knife is the maximum infliction of damage (through many severe wounds to cause a fatality—the more wounds, the better in terms of outcome). Again, any employment of the knife by police requires the officer to not only articulate the factors known to him in order to justify that deadly force response *for each wound,* but also to make that justification plain to those who will be judging his actions and behavior. Teaching an officer to inflict "maximum damage to rapidly de-animate the suspect" is simply irresponsible within the police mission—compliance is the goal of any responsible deadly force training whether through firearms or the use of the knife.

Training should include *when* the knife might reasonably and legally be employed. While deadly force is always "deadly force" regardless of the instrument, there are larger political ramifications to the use of a knife as a deadly weapon by an officer. The purpose of the police knife as a weapon is to save the officer's or another's life, to stop the offender's deadly attack, and to permit the officer to escape from the immediate situation in order to transition to other, more "traditional" *police* weapons if the deadly force threshold remains. For these reasons (as well as others), training should emphasize that the deadly force response with tactical folding knife is permitted only in the last-ditch defense of self or others, when a firearm or other means is not available. Training involving knife employment solutions primarily involves weapon retention problems because that is generally the situation in which officers have, in the past, employed the knife as deadly force.

This training, *emphasizing* a realistic law enforcement orientation through valid, incident-specific training with constitutional, legal, and policy restrictions built in, result in a police response that is defensible. For example, a trained officer's response to a very desperate situation was:

- 2003: An officer is on his back, with a skilled suspect "cross-mounted" on top of him. The officer is losing his handgun, and according to his training in the last-ditch defense of life with a knife, he deploys the knife and yells, "Stop, or I'll stab you!" The suspect looks over his shoulder, realizes that he is being given a choice: stop fighting and comply immediately, or take a possibly fatal stab wound. With no real option, the suspect instantly makes the "smart" decision, and is safely taken into custody—unharmed.

This "trained" response by a police officer (not a soldier or martial artist) mirrored perfectly the training he had received:

- He recognized through his training that he was losing this deadly fight.
- He was able to protect his handgun well enough that he could safely access his knife.
- He was able to competently and safely access his knife, deploying it.
- He was able to recognize that he could safely warn the suspect to "Stop or I'll stab you!"
- He was able to recognize compliance by the suspect in time to prevent the need for a deadly force response.
- He was also able to safely disengage from the suspect, then waited for a backup officer as trained before cuffing the suspect.

This officer stated that if the suspect had not stopped on the first warning, he would have employed the knife as a deadly weapon. This, too, was per his training, and would have been objectively reasonable if the suspect had not complied. Every instance where a trained officer resorts to a knife to save his or her life cannot be expected to be a "bloodless save." The properly trained officer, having been trained in a *police-oriented* deadly force response course, will be more likely to achieve defensible and reasonable conduct.

Conclusion

When is a tool a weapon? When that tool is used as a weapon. Hammer. Screwdriver. Baseball bat. Crow bar. Knife. All innocuous tools or sports equipment. Each extremely useful for that which it was designed. And each has resulted in a justified shooting by an officer of an offender who threatened an officer's life with that "tool" employed as a "deadly weapon."

Cops carry knives. They do so primarily for utility, as well as a method of last-ditch defense of life. While administrators (and society) recognize the utilitarian aspects of a knife, few recognize—or wish to recognize—the very real secondary intent that officers have for on-duty knife carry. Because the knife is both a tool and a weapon, officers need realistic policy direction and training inhibiting primitive behavior (driven by an intense survival need) in defense of life, and encourages the officer's limited employment during a last-ditch deadly force response.

Policy should provide guidance for utility purposes, and for the last-ditch employment of the knife for defense. Type(s) of knives, number, style, etc., that officers may possess, as well as requirements to avoid alarming behavior (such as repeatedly flipping the knife open and closed in public—yes, that has occurred more than once and in different parts of the country) should be a part of the policy. The recognition of the knife as an instrument in "last-ditch" option for defense (not "last resort," carrying with that language the intrinsic requirement of having attempted every other force option in a situation that is dynamic, life-threatening, and tense, uncertain, and rapidly evolving") should be formally codified in policy.

Training should avoid martial arts or military philosophies or solutions. There should be absolutely no emphasis on "knife-fighting" or any concepts or drills involving the repetition of techniques of "maximum infliction of damage" or "de-animation" of the suspect. These concepts are alien to police work, and should be avoided.

Instead, a situation-based training based on the US Constitution, law, and policy, espousing a limited employment of the knife is what is needed to prepare each officer to survive a deadly force situation where officers in the past have been severely injured or murdered. It will likely center around weapon retention situations where the officer is alone, fatigued, being overpowered, possibly injured, and in desperate fear for his life. The officer is trained to employ the knife a limited method that is simultaneously effective. This training additionally provides the officer with the ability to articulate how desperate the situation was and why the knife was needed to save his or her life.

Instead of ignoring the knife, agencies and the administrators might benefit by publishing a policy that guides their officer's actions, and then training the officers in order to inhibit the human's natural primitive behavior when it comes to saving his life with an edged weapon. This training will prepare officers to defend their lives in a defensible fashion that not only limits their liability—and that of their agency's, but also may save their life.

A free model Duty Knife policy is available from Cutting Edge Training, LLC. Request it by e-mail at gtwilliams@cuttingedgetraining.org.

George T. Williams is the Director of Training for *CUTTING EDGE TRAINING, L.L.C.,* in Bellingham, Washington. He has been a trainer of police since 1981, and full-time since 1987. Mr. Williams, a certified Police Master Instructor, is responsible for the development and presentation of unique and revolutionary police training programs. He certifies instructors in Defensive Tactics, impact weapons, and shooting. His experience in training law enforcement ranges from police academies, through municipal and county agencies to the state and federal government level. A SWAT tactics and weapons trainer, he has been a consultant to several dozen teams in the Western United States since 1985. As a Police Training Specialist, he has personally trained officers from all 50 States and several U.S. Territories, as well officers from 14 foreign countries. Mr. Williams also serves as a policy and training advisor to several law enforcement agencies throughout the United States.

Author. He is a frequent contributor to various national police magazines with over 160 articles published. He also authored and co-authored a series of articles detailing the facts leading to the murders of California officers from 1980 to 1998, directly influencing the course content of academies and advanced officer training. Mr.

Williams was a core member for the California P.O.S.T. Committee for the Study of Law Enforcement Officers Killed and Assaulted (LEOKA), and continues his study of the causes of officer murders on an informal basis. He is also the author of one book, "Force Reporting for Every Cop," published by Jones & Barlett Publishers, 2006.

Expert Witness and Litigation Consultant. Mr. Williams serves as a risk management consultant and Expert Witness defending officers in civil rights litigation of officer-involved use of force, tactics, and procedures since 1991. He has successfully served nationally in this capacity since 1991, in federal and superior criminal and civil courts. Mr. Williams provides deposition and trial preparation services to police agencies nationwide, assisting officers to achieve the most comprehensive testimony possible.

Contact him by e-mail at: _gtwilliams@cuttingedgetraining.org,_ or by phone: 360.671.2007.

THE SLAUGHTER OF INNOCENTS. UNDERSTANDING THE FIVE PHASES OF THE ACTIVE SHOOTER

by Lt. Dan Marcou

You are attending a lecture in an auditorium of a local College, where you are taking classes to complete your master's degree. You are an off duty police officer seated in the audience listening to a presentation on community policing by a highly esteemed professor, when suddenly a heavily armed man in dressed in black bursts through the door of the auditorium and opens fire with a pump action 12 gauge shotgun.

The auditorium transforms from the picture of decorum to bloody chaos immediately due to this ultimate act of terrorism. The killing is not for a country, it is not for a cause, it is not for Allah, nor even on behalf of a domestic radical group. The killing is for one thing and one thing only, "achieving a top score."

You are already on the move, before the killer has fired his first shot. The shooter is oblivious to your presence, because he has an entire auditorium full of victims that he has turned into a swirling twirling mass of confusion and he is experiencing tunnel vision. He is in the midst of his twisted ecstasy.

You are on the move, being careful to stay beyond his peripheral vision and you have thankfully chosen to be defiant. Your college has declared its campus a gun free zone and has made the carrying of a firearm to your class an act, which could lead to your expulsion even though you are a full time police officer. You have chosen to follow your department's policy and disregard the college's mandate.

You move quickly to a position of advantage and take careful aim with your off duty Glock. You have been trained in "Responding to an Active Shooter." You have prepared by training with your off duty weapon. You do not identify yourself. You do not ask him to drop the gun. You take careful aim and fire once. Your bullet enters the suspect's left ear, expands and severs the brain stem, lodging against the skull on the opposite side of the entrance wound. The killer crumples instantly lifeless before he hits the floor.

There are casualties, but because you know how to save lives as well as end them, you immediately apply pressure to the wounds of the injured and direct aid calmly to your location with your cell phone. No one dies except the shooter, who has now, thanks to you discovered, whether or not there is a hell for people who shoot kill innocents. He has had his question answered. The answer is yes. He has also learned there are no virgins for the murderers of innocents, no exercise hour, no television, no conjugal visits, no cafeteria and no parole.

Obstacles

There are some truths to the fictional account you have just read. Police Officers are more prepared than ever to respond to the ever growing phenomenon of the Active Shooter. Training is available and is being attended by officers all over the country. Legislators have made it easier than ever for highly trained officers, who are on duty and off duty as well as retired to carry concealed weapons and possibly be in a position to do something in the event of an active shooter.

Colleges, which have become targets, have mandated with their own rules and regulations the disarming of those, who could and would protect them if this death and destruction were visited upon them. Some colleges all over the nation have their police and security patrolling "unarmed." The college administrations write rules and regulations that if followed to the letter would disarm police officers attending classes at their facility.

Trainers are experiencing cases where college police attempt to attend active shooter classes and SWAT classes, but are blocked by deans who over-see college police and security. The college administrators feel that these classes will create an overbearing and heavy handed police force on campus. They do this in the wake of the deaths on campuses at Blacksburg, De Kalb and even the University of Montreal in Canada..

Mental health professionals are routinely failing to properly diagnose the degree of danger many persons, who are mentally ill. Many officers have stories of the subjects who they put a mental holds on, who were immediately released by mental health professionals. Shortly thereafter the subjects went out and killed. The irony is in many of these cases, after the killing, when the subject is about to be tried for their crimes, the same mental health professionals, now enlightened, will diagnose the same subject, as too mentally ill to stand trial.

In spite of these obstacles law enforcement continues to prepare for the active shooter. Agencies are now aware that they do not have to wait until the crying and the dying starts to intervene effectively in these cases of the active shooter. Rolling out the yellow crime scene tape is not the only option for law enforcement.

Five Phases of the Active Shooter

A simple view of the active shooter was developed and is being trained by Lt. Dan Marcou retired from the La Crosse, Wisconsin Police Department. He developed the program while working for the La Crosse Police Department and was able to apply the philosophy with real world success. One of the successes earned Officer Bob Michalski and Lt. Marcou the Associate of SWAT Personnel Officers of the Year in 2004 for their response to an active shooter, who was killing innocents with an Uzi in a hotel in Oak Creek Wisconsin.

In the discussion of the active shooter "he" will be utilized, because generally these are males, but the killing of innocents in not a male-only club any more. The five phases of the active shooter are:

The Fantasy Stage

During the fantasy stage the shooter pictures himself doing the shooting. He fantasizes about the headlines he will receive. The shooter might draw pictures of the event and make web site postings. They have been known to write stories about the shootings and turn them into schools for a grade. Often they predict, promise and warn people about the impending event. If law enforcement is notified in advance and takes actions there is a strong possibility tragedy will be averted with zero casualties.

Planning Stage

In this stage the subject is deciding on the, who what when where and how of his joyful killing spree. They most often will put their plans down in writing. They will decide the time and location of the event and what weapons they will need to carry out the carnage. They will design their response to inflict as much death and suffering as possible. They may prepare a shopping list of items needed to carry out the plan.

The shooter will determine how to travel to the location and how to conceal their weapons. They will decide on whether to commit the crime alone, or to confide in and utilize an accomplice. The internet affords the opportunity for dangerously unstable persons to communicate.

If a family member, friend, teacher, school liaison or anyone else discovers the plans, and notifies the police officer have an opportunity to intervene before the event with once again zero casualties.

Preparation Stage

During this stage the suspect will buy, beg, borrow and steal items that they need for the event. They might buy guns, and ammo. They might purchase materials for explosives, which when observed separately look innocuous, but when combined are deadly. They often steal what they cannot buy. This often is done by stealing from family members.

They will assemble their improvised explosive devices and train with their weapons. They may detonate some explosives to insure that they will work.

The active shooters will visit the sites they will attack and do drawings and schematics of the areas. They will conduct reconnaissance as if they are preparing for a military operation.

The potential shooter might be arrested by police after they receive a call from a friend, family member, or suspicious citizen. The potential shooter might be apprehended by an alert officer, after a traffic stop or during an in progress theft or burglary. If done with caution and alertness the suspect can be taken into custody with zero casualties.

Approach Stage

The closer to the event, the more dangerous it will be, when officers take action. When the subject is approaching the target he will be very dangerous, because he has his eyes on the prize. He has made his plans, armed himself and he has made his decision to kill. He may be walking, riding, or driving to the target, carrying his implements of death.

Officers might be prompted to contact the subject, because of the sheer alertness of an officer, or as a result of a traffic stop by an officer practicing interdiction. A citizen might make a call of a suspicious person.

The officer or officers making contact, during the approach stage are in danger, but as long as the officer(s) keep an open mind on every stop they can be kept safe by their superior tactics, skills and will to survive. There is a fine line between an officer having their name etched into an award or their name etched into a wall. This contact handled in a tactically sound manner can save many lives, prevent carnage, and end in there may be zero casualties.

Implementation Stage

When the active shooter opens fire immediate action needs to be taken. The ingredient that ties all of these incidents together is the active shooter will continue to shoot until they run out of victims, ammunition, or they are stopped by their own hand or an effective efficient act of courage.

The sooner an honorable gun fighter in the guise of an on duty officer, an off duty officer, an armed retired officer, an armed security guard the less funerals there will be. People ask how many should you have before you advance. The answer to this question could be answered by the potential victims, who are about to succumb to the mad man's desire to achieve "Top score." The potential victims would say, "six is better than five, five is better than four, four is better than three, three is better than two, two is better than one and one honorable gunfighter is better than none."

There is an old cavalry adage that goes, when the battle begins and you do not know what to do, "Ride to the sound of the guns."

A police officer has the following advantage:

- They are highly trained, honorable gun fighters.

- The active shooter will be focused on their dastardly deed.

- They will be creating a scene that will be loud and chaotic, and the perfect diversion.

- The initial responder(s) can use the chaos to identify the location of the shooter.

- The initial responder can use the chaos to move quietly to a position of advantage.

- Terrified victims will be able to direct officers to the location of the shooter.

- If the shooter is located in the act of shooting, officers do not have to verbalize they can take the shot and make the shot.

- If the shooter is contained by the actions of the officers in a non-violent pose, officers may initiate a classic SWAT response.

On Duty Tactics

Officers responding to a call of an active shooter must realize they have been thrust into a position that calls for decisive action and what they decide to do can save lives and minimize casualties.

Training can help prepare the first responding officers for the moment they arrive at the scene of such an incident. This is a dire situation and we may take casualties. A key decision has to be made instantaneously and that is whether to contain and await other units, or move to contact, because defenseless citizens that the officer is sworn to protect are dying with each shot.

When the first responding officer arrives they should remember to use long guns for long halls. Officers should choose to put superior fire power into their hands. Breathe and try to control the heart rate on the approach as you use your radio on the move, directing additional units en route and notifying others of the actions you are taking.

Do not throw your life away, breathe, think, advance, using the chaos as your diversion. You may have to pass wounded, conduct quick interviews on the move and encourage direct fleeing individuals to continue their flight, while you advance on the shooter.

Gather as much information as possible and then attempt to move to a position of advantage that affords a field of vision, clear shot and cover if at all possible. Attempt to do this without alerting the suspect of your presence.

Quickly assess the actions of the suspect and if he is in the act of shooting, and endangering innocents of death and or great bodily harm, you need not advise warn or request. You may take the shot and make the shot. Then break up your tunnel vision and look for additional shooters. Communicate your location and actions and reload in the lull. This should be done while covering the downed suspect. Secure the suspect and assess his condition.

Off Duty Tactics

As you read this you either carry off duty or you do not. If you carry off duty ask yourself these questions:

- ✓ Do I carry a weapon and holster I have trained with?,
- ✓ Do I have a way to identify myself as a police officer?
- ✓ Do I have a way to secure a suspect I have arrested off duty?
- ✓ Do I have a way to communicate off duty?
- ✓ Do I have reload capability?
- ✓ Have I participated in hands on "Active Shooter Response" training.
- ✓ Have I read and digested my agency's off duty policy and deadly force policy?

If you answered no to any of these questions you need to take some kind of action to answer yes.

If you do not carry off-duty, take the time to ask the following:

- ✓ Should I carry off duty in a post 9-11 post Columbine world?
- ✓ If someone was shooting in my child's school would I take action armed or not?
- ✓ Do you possess empty hand deadly force options for the worst case scenario?
- ✓ If I was about to be shot by an active shooter would I refuse to go quietly into the night?

The Law

Due to changes in the federal law it is much easier for officers to carry concealed weapons off duty. Retired officers can also carry off duty, when they have received proper training and carry identification with departmental authorization. Officers should check their local policies and procedures, before arming themselves. Many agencies do not allow officers, who are retired to carry concealed weapons out of concerns for liability. Administrators should ask themselves if this is prudent in today's world.

Conclusion

Clearly this nation has not seen the last mindless homicidal act. It is a very real possibility that any police officer, on duty or off, regardless of their department size, rank, shift, or assignment might be faced with a suspect laying down a withering fire at innocent men women and children. These heartless killers might be a threat to you, your family or the people you are sworn to protect.

The location of your date with destiny might be a mall, a church, a court room, a school, a hotel, or even a police station. **Prepare!**

Author: Lt. Dan Marcou arrested his last felon in November 2006 after 33 years in Law Enforcement. He now is an extremely active police trainer. He is author of the highly acclaimed police novel, "The Calling. The Making of a Veteran Cop," which is available now through Amazon. com and Barnes and Noble on-line. To contact "Lt. Dan" to arrange for training or to purchase an autographed copy of his book, he can be reached at marcoudj@charter.net.

A DISCUSSION OF THE IMPORTANCE OF A HOLISTIC APPROACH TO THE TRAINING OF ATTITUDES AND MENTAL PREPAREDNESS IN POLICE OFFICERS

by Jim Dowle

It has been said of police training that we "Train officers as sprinters and yet expect them to run a marathon." An important contrast between a sprinter and a marathon runner is not just the obvious physical one, a greater part is in the differing mental attitudes.

As a police trainer in the UK, I have often tried to apply the models and principles of pure training to the role of a police officer. I have come to the conclusion that it is impossible to thoroughly train a patrol officer for the job he or she will have to do. We could spend thirty years training an officer to deal with every eventuality, then the call would come in that the Martians have landed in the parking lot and they would have have to make it up on the hoof!

In purest training terms it is not possible to complete a job analysis of the role. Therefore, complete training objectives that rely on accurate statements of the required performance in the various operational conditions, and achieved to a clear standard, cannot be guaranteed. Thankfully, the majority of good police trainers are more pragmatist than theorist. This leads to most police training regimes being designed to equip officers across a broad range of knowledge and skills, relying on the initiative of the officer to deal with the 'untrainable'. This approach is successful and adequate for most, as it relies on a thorough mix of knowledge and skills based training. However, the most vital element required of a police officer is something that neither knowledge or skills can help with, and that is attitude. The trainers reading this essay will be familiar with the three domains of learning; the *cognitive domain* dealing with facts, knowledge and understanding, the *psychomotor domain* relating to physical skills, and finally the *affective domain*, that relates to attitude and behaviour.

Setting and achieving objectives in the affective domain is a real challenge. The main reason for this is that SMART objectives (Specific, Measureable, Achievable, Relevant, Timely) are easy to observe in the cognitive and pyschomotor domains. We can set oral or written tests to check legal definitions. We can observe that driving, shooting and handcuffing skills are demonstrated to the required standard. What we cannot readily, and more importantly objectively, observe is whether a student officer demonstrates the correct attitudes or behaviour.

The way most training regimes get around this is by setting rules or examples of what is acceptable or unacceptable behaviour. Put another way a list of statements can be made that a person exhibiting the required behaviour will display certain traits (and there will follow a list of desired behaviours). Alternatively, a list of statements will be made in the negative sense, that is, a list of negative behaviours that would be observed in someone who is not suitable for the role. In the past , this has been done informally through 'Field Training', setting an experienced officer to train and observe a student officer. However, a lot of reliance was placed on the 'gut feeling' of the trainer and this consequently brings with it an element of subjectivity. Essentially though it is the gut feeling, that when examined and elucidated actually provides the statements required for comparison of behaviour. Many police trainers have the ability (due to their gut feeling) to pick out very quickly from a class of recruits, those that will not make it.

Attitude then, though difficult to define and set objectives for, is at the core of training for police officers. It is that single element that will create the required trust amongst their colleagues. After all, every team has someone whose skill with a firearm, or at the wheel of a car, occassioanlly falls below the required standard, whose knowledge of law and procedure is sadly lacking. However, when a team member falls below the standard in attitude, trust is lost, integrity is brought into question, and the officer will struggle to regain their position.

There is much written on the subjects of mental preparedness, emotional survival, police mindset and occupational pyschology, all having a bearing on attitude. Unfortunately, the work of these enlightened people is often neglected by the very organistaions that they are there to help. A common theme in all these subjects is the importance of training the mind of the officer from Day One to survive what the job may throw at them. I have discussed the inherent difficulty in the setting of objectives in the affective domain, and therein lies part of the problem. In today's target obsessed management culture, if it is difficult to set a target it is difficult to measure it and therefore difficult to demonstrate successful results. Ergo the management invest time and money in something that can be measured instead.

It is imperative that trainers do not take their eye off the ball and continue to develop the correct mental attitude in all their recruits.

This should start at the recruitment stage. If you are lucky enough to have influence over who is recruited, then some form of attitudinal filter* needs to be built in. Unfortunately many police departments are increasingly competing with the private sector for a limited pool of human resources. This, when added to recruiting targets, can often lead to a drop in standards. This is evidenced by reduced physical tests, lower academic attainment etc. These restrictions on the quality of individuals joining the job can be, and are being, absorbed into departments. However, the standard that absolutely cannot be relaxed is that of attitude.

It is not in the scope of this essay to discuss what these may be. There are many specialist sources and publications that can provide guidance in this area.

In our modern 'nanny' society where everyone is told that they are all equal and are all to be given the same opportunity, it is vital that we do not lose sight of the fact that not everyone is cut out to be a cop. In fact we may be causing serious pyschological harm to some people by relaxing standards and allowing them to experience some aspects of police work. That is why the importance of robust standards and objectives cannot be underestimated, nor can they be relaxed.

Many departments have a two-year probationary period that must be satisfactorily completed before an officer's appointment is confirmed. This is a useful period of time during which an individual officer's attitude can be observed. It is also, an excellent opportunity to develop the required attitude and mental outlook that will enable that officer to be an asset to their team and department. "Probation is your 'no-strings attached, guilt-free, no excuses needed, no questions asked, sorry about your luck, don't let the door hit you' way to prevent unsuitable people from becoming police officers. Since you yourself have already clearly defined exactly what 'unsuitable' means, and since the (training) process identified and documented just such a person, why would you ever give this person a pass? Start using probation for its real purpose. And be very glad you had this one last chance." However, as experienced trainers know, you will make no friends amongst the 'bean counters' and adminstrators by losing a recruit.

When an officer joins the police we owe it to them to be honest. There is no point dressing up the job, or playing down the seedier side. We owe it to our future colleagues to give them the reality pill and tell it how it is. This job is not for everyone, yet allsorts can make it as cops. We have to examine the motives of our recruits and if necessary put them straight. Many are attracted by the security and benefits package, many by the TV image. It is better to lose them now, than put them in a position where they may become a danger to themselves or their colleagues or suffer serious pyschological harm. This is particularly the case when a significant number of emotionally 'damaged' people apply to join the police in order to achieve a level of control within their own lives. Although this statement is anecdotal, it is based on the report that a significant numbers of officers are seeking counselling having been exposed to various unpleasant parts of police work, that has reminded them of their own past lives. It needs to be emphasised that we should not shirk our responsibilities by letting these people through the net. We have a duty of care to ensure all our officers are prepared to deal with what the job may throw at them. If it is a matter of targets and funding, then the dire cost of litigation when we get it wrong needs to be highlighted to the 'bean counters'.

Amongst the first elements that need to be trained are the imminent changes to the recruits own personality, the reactions of their friends and family, the importance of building a robust support structure and finally building a winning mindset. The importance of training, and to some extent warning officers of these factors is vital during the academy/college/initial training stage. The reason for this is as Kevin Gilmartin states in *Emotional Survival for Law Enforcment;* "They have so much to learn to become competent officers, most of which they learn from the older cops, the ones who have been there and done that. The reality is that although these more experienced officers really do know how to work the streets, often tragically, that's the only part of their lives that does work effectively." The reality is that without this warning, officers can find themselves becoming cynical, negative and downright angry, (like their tutors) as they strive to better their performance as a cop without understanding the importance of keeping a rounded personality and a healthy worldview. Friends, families and relationships can suffer if recruits remain ignorant of the inherent danger of totally focussing on police work. Ultimately we need our officers to have a rounded life with many strands to it. This will help them bounce back to normal performance when they face a stressful or difficult period in their future careers. Honesty is paramount with no 'gilding of the lily'. The training that I have developed in my own force to brief recruits on the potential pitfalls of a police career does just that. Recently one recruit (an ex-primary school teacher) approached his trainers and asked to resign. Following these sessions he had considered carefully the impact that police work would have on his relationship with his own young family and decided that he did not want to expose himself to the 'dirty' world. Better now, at fourteen weeks, than later down the line. This ex-recruit had my complete support and won my deep respect for his honesty to himself and his colleagues.

As I have argued, the importance of mentally preparing recruits to deal with people at their "maddest, baddest and saddest" *Gilmartin 2002* and the potential negativity that it can cause is one thing, however, this needs to be balanced with a positive message. This is where the building blocks of mental preparation that form the foundation of officer survival are laid.

From the first days of an officer's service it is necessary to develop a positive, winning mindset. "You must decide right now, that no matter what, you will win a deadly force encounter. Your most critical survival weapon is not hanging on your gun belt; it's between your ears. A determined and winning attitude will keep you alive and you need to cultivate that determination now – and keep it forever." *Artwohl & Christensen 1997*. This can be done in a number of ways, however, a holistic approach should be taken. This prevents the potential for mixed or conflicting messages to be given. For example the concept of "Hypervigilance – the necessary manner of viewing the world from a threat-based perspective, having the mindset to see the events unfolding as potentially hazardous." *Gilmartin 2002* can potentially cause incomprehension for inexperienced officers. That is, on the one hand they are warned of the potentially negative effects of the "Hypervigilance biological rollercoaster" *Gilmartin 2002*, yet on the other hand they are told that they must demonstrate hypervigilance in order to ensure the correct mental attitude to achieve good officer safety. A thorough understanding of the models is necessary by all trainers involved in the delivery of these subjects in order that they can properly elucidate the facts and minimise confusion.

Trainers need to inspire recruits to start their own training in their first few days of service. To train their own minds in preparation for the day when they will face conflict. To question themselves so that when they are weighed and measured on the field of conflict, they will not be found wanting. To look themselves in the eyes and be honest with their inner self. Ultimately they must ask themselves the question; Will I win? The answer has to be 'YES'. Any other answer should lead to another career path. "Some would argue that since everyone in basic training receives the same exposure to mental preparation and conditioning this may not be the deciding factor. The difference, however, lies with commitment, responsibility and control. The training staff at basic academies has control over training as they determine what drills will be conducted, how many repetitions of any given skill will be performed, what information will be presented during the academic sessions, and what exercises the students will participate in. What they do not control is what goes on in the mind of the individual officer. The mind is the most powerful weapon an officer has yet it is not issued by the agency and cannot be inspected by the range master or armourer. There is no owner's manual or manufacturer's guarantee. However, inside the mind of trainees lies the key to unlocking the warrior spirit within them" *Willis 2006*. It is not possible to look inside the mind of trainees, but it is possible to develop the winning mind. This is not 'Gung Ho' pysching up for sport or a show of confidence. This is about preparing one's inner spirit, and being comfortable with the choice. Carl Jung said that human instincts "belong to a 'collective unconcious' because they exist independantly of the individual psyche and contain universally recognised, inherited aspects." *Jung 1991*. Aggression is one of these instincts, and that needs to be controlled and understood by recruits from early on. It then needs to be honed, developed and controlled like any other desireable quality, such as empathy, resilience and negotiation. It can then be used in a controlled way, just like any other tool in an officer's communication toolkit. Anyone who has ever seen the New Zealand Allblacks perform the *Haka* will know what a true demonstration of self-confidence and controlled aggression looks like, and how terrifying it can be to an opponent. I am not recommending officers emulate this on the street, but it serves as a good example!

I have often found that the famous, sheep, wolves and sheepdogs analogy works well with recruits. As they learn through the simple parallels of *sheep* (The majority of society who just want to do their own thing, bring up their young, and get fat off the land), *wolves*, (A minority of predators, criminals and other law-breaking outsiders), and the *sheepdogs* (The police, who are seen by the sheep as being similar to wolves, who keep them from breaking the rules and running amok, who are generally resented by the sheep except when the wolves come to town). I have found that this helps instill a little pride in recruits and helps them to realise that they are now different, that they have chosen a special path and they too are now predators, but with the best of intentions.

It is imperative to give recruits the self-confidence to face situations of conflict with not only self-belief, but with the instincts to know that they will win the encounter. This can be through negotiation, calming a situation down using tactical communications while awaiting back-up, or ultimately using officer safety skills and techniques, with or without weapons. The role of trainers here is many faceted. It is not just about educating the recruits and training them in officer safety skills. It is about relating the classroom or dojo to reality, attempting, as far as possible to recreate the reality of situations that an officer may face. "People are much more likely to feel high levels of fear or even panic when they are unprepared to deal with a threat. The actual threat is not nearly as important as the level of preparation. The more prepared you are, the more in control you feel, and the less fear you will experience. It's important that deadly force training be as realistic as possible and that it programs you to win." *Artwohl & Christensen 1997.* This means not just investing time and money in selecting realistic venues, but recreating as far as possible the fear and dynamism that occurs in a 'real' incident. It is here the recruit starts to build the automatic, trained responses.

If an officer experiences in training an element of the stresses they will experience in a real 'life or death' situation, we can to some extent inoculate the officer against fear. Artwohl and Christensen cover the concept of Stress Inoculation Training (SIT). "Once you understand all the physical, cognitive, perceptual and emotional changes caused by the biochemistry of the high arousal state, you will not fear them, be confused by them, or be distracted by them." *Artwohl & Christensen 1997.* The benefit of this can be illustrated by the following example of a well trained and mentally prepared cop who found himself in a bank that was being robbed by a gang of four men, two of whom were armed with AR-15s. "I heard a lot of gunfire and watched the walls exploding by me as the rounds from the other three guys were hitting the Sheetrock. It was kind of strange, but once they started shooting, I wasn't scared anymore because all of a sudden I felt like a had a duty to protect the people in the bank. I really can't explain it . but I was thinking about those people and about what I had to do to take out the bad guys." *Klinger 2004.*

There are other well documented examples of how officers revert to training when the chips are down and they are fighting for their lives. We owe it to our officers to ensure that the training that they revert to is fit for purpose, and that it prepares them for the realities of close combat, not some politically correct vision of what a higher authority thinks will be acceptable to an ever critical media. Simple drills need to be practised and repeated by rote until a robust muscle memory is achieved. Recruits need to understand the impact of stress on their fine motor skills. I will never forget the lesson taught me by a retired Royal Marine when he saw me on the range thumbing the slide release catch on my Sig P226. He told me about a gunfight in which he had been involved whilst working on an American close-protection team in a hotel lobby in Egypt. He noticed mid-battle that his partner had stopped firing and when the firefight was over he looked over to check him and saw him staring incredulously at his gun hand. The top slide was locked back and his partner's right thumb was wagging ineffectually near the slide release catch. He hadn't fired a round since his first reload, but due to his loss of fine motor skills he had not managed to release the top slide, and because he was operating under extreme stress he had not had the time or desire to think of an alternative method of releasing it. He felt betrayed by his own body and just could not move. He then demonstrated to me the correct method by gripping the top slide with his weak hand and punching his gun hand forward. I re-trained myself over weeks of dry drills, and have never thumbed a slide release catch since! The use of anecdotal examples is useful as many students have reported to me over the years that they remember a lesson better when it is illustrated by an actual 'story' or experience. (Obvisously without the session becoming a trainer's war stories).

Part of this process is debunking some of the myths and taking away a student's fear of the unknown. It is not uncommon in this day and age to find yourself training someone who has never really faced physical assault. This is due to the diminishing involvement in schools and colleges of playing team sports. It is quite conceivable now that the police recruits training for the harsh realities of life have never been in a rugby scrum or been the victim of a particularly hard tackle in a game of football. That is why we ensure our recruits at least know how they are going to react to a punch in the face (albeit by a fist-suited opponent) before they hit the streets! Another part of dealing with a fear of the unknown is briefing recruits on exactly how they will feel. This has the advantage for the recruit of recognising something as familiar when it happens to them. This element of training is often skimmed over, or worse, left out altogether from training programs that require space for more 'politically sensitive' subjects. However, the potentially disastrous repercussions on an officer's future emotional and pyschological welfare of not investing time in this training should never be underestimated.

There is no area of police work where the mental preparation for the aftermath of using force in conflict is more imperative than that of *deadly force*. This is where the fragile balance between an officer's perception of right and wrong can greatly affect someone who has not thoroughly prepared for the possibility of it happening to them. After all, police officers generally join the job to help people not to kill them. This complete contradiction of deeply seated principles against necessary actions is a double bind and can be the undoing of many a good cop. I read somewhere that around 80% of American cops who have killed in the line duty suffer some form of psychological illness after the event. I have to say I am not surprised. I have met many police officers and soldiers who have killed in the line of duty and I am humbled by their shared humility. Some have suffered greatly at the hands of incompetent administrators, misunderstanding commanders and ill-informed lawyers. Some have questioned their own strongly held beliefs and found it hard to look their loved ones in the eye. Some have been absolutely fine. There is no checklist of common after-shooting reactions. There is, however, an absolute necessity to train all officers to prepare for the possible stress reactions they may experience when they use deadly force. This must include building the winning mindset in order that officers know there is a liklihood that they will get injured during the gunfight, and that even if they do, they MUST still win it! I remember walking out of a SWAT training session because of an argument with an inexperienced instructor. I was younger and more hot-headed than I am today and I threw my teddy in the corner. We were rehearsing rapid room entry drills against barricaded suspects. I was the first into the room and the instructor palmed me on the shoulder and said "Go down you're hit!." I refused and quietly explained that the first thing I would do if I was hit was to neutralise the threat. That was my mindset that I had mentally rehearsed to myself over and over, since joining the army reserve years ago. He said "If you're hit you go down so the next man can engage the threat." You can imagine how the rest of the converstaion went, him falling back on his position as instructor, me being too bloody minded to accept his flawed teaching. The point is we must train our recruits to fight through injury and win, before they concern themselves with how badly they are hurt. After all, there may not be a 'next man'.

There are many publications that deal with this subject in a competent way and I can not even brush the surface in the context of this brief essay. The important point is that this preparation should be done in a joined-up manner. The subjects of fear, perceptual distortion, post traumatic stress disorder (PTSD), the aftermath of shootings, the legal processes and the support to the officers and their families, need to be hard-wired to the previously mentioned topics. If they are not, our recruits will spot the gaps as easily as you would spot a police chief doing under-cover surveillance.

On the subject of PTSD, in the UK we are moving away from Critical Incident Debriefing. We are using a process called called TRiM (Trauma Risk Management). It was developed by the British Army and following a succesful trial in the Royal Marines for debriefing of Combat Stress and PTSD, it is being rolled out throughout the army. Several police forces, including my own, are now using TRiM. It differs from Critical Incident Debriefing, because it is not a counselling session, nor is it carried out by health-care professionals. It is based on the principles of education, risk assessment and mentoring. It is a peer assessment carried out by specially trained police officers who can identify whether the subject of the assessment is at risk of developing some form of pyschological condition or whether they will 'get over it' in due course. If there are potential problems identified a referral to a relevant professional can be made. I have described it in simplistic terms, however, it is very effective and its great strength is that officers are much happier talking to a colleague than to a 'shrink'!

I have touched the surface of a number of elements of mental preparedness training for police officers. Overall any police training program needs to include a wide range of attitudinal objectives, with the overall aim being to provide a holistic approach to mental preparedness. All elements that I have mentioned need to be included, inter-linked and inter-related. The endstate will be an officer who leaves the academy with a realistic expectation of the way they will be perceived by society; the different outlook they will have on life; the dignity of the path that they have chosen; the dangers of negativity and cynicism and the importance of maintaining a balanced worldview; the incentive to build a winning mindset in the way of the warrior; the commitment to train themselves every day to develop their own mental robustness and resilience; the ablity to anticipate fear and recognise its effects, to turn these to their own benefit and use the effects positively; the foresight to predict the way their body will react should they use deadly force and the likely reactions of those around them; the honesty to recognise their own reactions to stress and seek help when it is hard to cope; and finally, the mindset that they are one of the 'good guys', they are strong, and they will win. It is a big ask.

Bibliography

Artwhol, Alexis and Christensen, Loren W. *"Deadly Force Encounters: What Cops Need to Know to Mentally Prepare for and Survive a Gunfight."* Paladin Press 1997

Gilmartin, Kevin M. *"Emotional Survival for Law Enforcemnet – A guide for officers and their families"* E-S Press, 2002

Jung, Carl G. *"The Archytypes and the Collective Unconcious, The Collected Works of C G Jung"* Routledge, 1991

Klinger, David. *"Into the Kill Zone. A Cop's Eye View of Deadly Force."* Jossey-Bass, 2004

Sanow, Ed. *"Probation's Catch & Release Program"* Law and Order Magazine, Hendon Publishing, December 2007

Willis, Brian. *"Winning Mind, Warrior Spirit, Cop Body"* The Law Enforcement Executive Forum, July/August 2006

"Trauma Risk Management – Critical Incidents, Dealing with your Reactions." Hertfordshire Constabulary, 2006

Jim Dowle is a serving police sergeant in Hertfordshire Constabualry. He has served for almost eighteen years in mainly frontline uniform roles, eleven years of which as a member of the Tactical Firearms Team, specialising as a sniper and close protection officer.

In 2000 he secured a UK Government research project investigating the effects of snipers shooting through glass. He travelled extensively during this work, conducting research and presenting his findings, as well as gaining the opportunity to train with diverse law enforcement and military units, for example the Royal Marines, the FBI Academy, GSG9, Dallas PD SWAT, The Royal Ulster Constabulary and the Lethal Force Institute. He is now considered an authority in this subject and holds a Master's Degree in Terminal Ballistics from the UK Defence Academy (formerly the Royal Military College of Science). A former member of ASLET, and the American Sniper Association, Jim has presented at several conferences in the US including ASLET, Sniperweek and the National Sniper/SWAT Symposium.

In 2003, Jim moved to the Force Training Department where he developed a unique Counter-Terrorism course which won the 2006 UK National Training Award. In 2007 he was invited to act as Judge and Ambassador for the UK awards. He currently writes the Terrorism Column for 'Law and Order' magazine and is a regular contibuter to the UK police press. He has developed mental preparedness and emotional survival training in his Force which is seen as a pioneer in the UK for these subjects. He is currently developing a research project with the University of Hertfordshire and King's College London to investigate the pyschological impact of sniper shootings.

12 TIPS TO IMPLEMENT A NEW PARADIGM IN YOUR "DEFENSIVE" TACTICS PROGRAM

by Tom Gillis CPO, BAJS

As I travel to different courses and seminars I see a common thread amongst warrior trainers, lack of training. On countless occasions I've met trainers from different departments across the world that have been thrust into their position and not been adequately prepared. When this occurs one of the most serious consequences is that recruits do not get the training they need and can subsequently be set up for failure. Often these trainers have no idea that they're not equipping their officers with the tools necessary to be successful. Many administrators, coaches, and trainers may truly believe that they are providing the most desirable training, and are likely honest hard workers themselves. So what then can we do to fix this problem?

The problem may be with the defensive tactics program itself. Many of these programs are designed with the wrong mindset in place. This mindset follows the trainers and in turn is passed onto the officers whose lives they touch. So just what is the "wrong" mindset? What exactly is wrong with many of our current "defensive tactics" (DT) programs?

The problem starts with the word "defensive." What is "defensive" about police work? Officers "defend" the public by "controlling" the offenders, subjects, and situations. This idea of being "defensive" starts right at the outset of these training programs and then saturates the training all the way through. From the outset officers are taught to defend themselves in an altercation instead of controlling the situation, the persons involved, and utilizing violence, power, and explosiveness to their advantage. Allow me to demonstrate my point with some illustrations.

- In a current training program in the U.S. trainers wanted to implement force on force scenario training. In order to implement the training without injuring recruits or quarries they placed two lines on the floor two meters apart from each other. Quarries were not permitted to cross their line, and likewise with the recruits. This means that if a recruit decides that it's appropriate to respond with baton strikes he has to strike the air to simulate that use of force.

  In this instance what is the recruit learning? How to strike air? Some trainers might make the argument that they're learning how to recognize a particular subject category and make a decision to respond. Can't this be done through the use of video?

- Again from our brothers in the U.S., one state standard for recruits is 16 hours of defensive tactics training. Six of these 16 hours must be classroom based. Again I ask you, what are these recruits being taught? Remember this is a state standard for every police agency. This means that every officer in that particular state is only receiving 10 mandatory hours of physical defensive tactics training.

- A Provincial Sheriffs Department in Canada completely changed its defensive tactics program. The amount of training was doubled. Officers were taught to think offensively and to be the predator in any altercation. Force on force simulation training was implemented. However the firearms program remained the same as it always had been where officers are taught to qualify rather then to gunfight. Officers spend all the time on the range shooting with one eye closed in order to score their shots at up to 15 yards. There is no movement to cover or support hand shooting. There is no marker cartridge scenario training. After over a year of the simulation training being implemented into the defensive tactics program the firearms training still hasn't been changed and now many of the elements of the DT program have begun to revert back to the way they were.

These are just three examples of the current state of defensive tactics training for many agencies. Very few agencies have made their way past this type of training to truly equip officers with the skills they need to save their lives when necessary. So the question begs to be asked, what can we do about it? Below I've offered 12 suggestions to the trainer officer to ensure their brothers and sisters of the shield receive the knowledge, skills, and mindset required to be successful in a law enforcement career.

1. Stop using the word "defensive." Starting immediately, if you haven't already done so, draft a proposal to your agency heads to change the name of your program to "Control Tactics." Why the name change? This simple little thing sends

the message to every recruit that they are expected to take control of subjects and situations, not defend themselves. When people hear the word "control" it conjures an image of officers taking the initiative in confrontations to control the subject, witnesses, crowd, and any other element of the confrontation.

2. Stop using the phrase "Officer Survival." This over used little phrase conjures up images of officers getting their asses kicked, but it's okay because they survived. In this line of work survival is not enough. Replace such phrases with "winning." Officers should be encouraged to think like a predator. Not in terms of seeking the weak prey but in terms of training like a predator, practicing skills, utilizing small unit (i.e. pack) tactics, utilizing weapons and sensitive targets, and, when appropriate, striking with ferocity until the threat is neutralized. Phrases like "Winning Mind," "Predator Mentality," "Warrior Spirit," and "Ferocity of Action," tell trainees that it's okay to use violence to hurt someone to control them; that it's appropriate to initiate the use of force once a determination about a subject is reached. These phrases tell the recruit that it's only acceptable to win an altercation, and that survival is a by-product of winning, not the other way around.

3. Your control tactics program should be no less then 80 hours in length and should include handcuffing techniques, empty hand fighting, ground fighting, empty hand lethal force/CQC (Close Quarter Combat), intermediate weapons, firearms retention, joint manipulation, pressure

points, and takedowns. There should also be a minimum of 4 hours of force on force simulation training including lethal force scenarios where recruits are permitted to make mistakes and then correct them during the scenario. This should be followed by another 4 hours of evaluation. Ultimately several days of force-on-force training would be desirable but for agencies on a tight budget and time restraint no less then the eight suggested is acceptable. Eighty hours is enough time to include a class room element where video presentations and lectures are provided. Firearms and control tactics should be merged so that instructors from each discipline are on the same page and teaching the same tactics, techniques, and mindset. Firearms training should focus on an actual gun fight and not qualifying. Most of the training should focus on winning a lethal force encounter and trainees should be educated in the physiology and psychology of combat. Any less then 80 hours isn't enough to cover all the elements of a program and do them justice.

4. Focus more on dynamic skills then static drills. Teach the officers how to apply the skills they've been taught in various and dynamic situations. This means that once officers have completed enough static drills to perform the technique with a minimum level of skill all the drills should be dynamic where officers are using their skills in simulated scenarios with their partners. This begins to move the officers' mind set away from skill based and begins to teach them how to apply their skills in a simulated application. Stress inoculation drills should be built into your training

to teach the trainee how to perform the skill under a high level of emotional stress. This also allows recruits to experiment with fixes to a problem and learn transition drills to and from different force options.

5. Become goal orientated. Too many programs focus on the techniques of the program and not the goal it's designed to reach. This means that if your officers are able to apply the skills just enough to get the job done, then that's fine. Becoming goal oriented encourages your officers to improvise and problem solve on their own. You may also consider implementing a 2 prong view to examinations. A written and practical exam can evaluate the basic skills and articulation and a second goal using a force-on-force scenario exam can measure goal orientation.

6. Teach the principles of the technique. For example there are several different ways to manipulate the joints in human limbs to reach a desired result. When teaching joint manipulation for example, teach the officers why and how the technique works and how it can be modified for various situations. Once the recruit has the basic idea they can be provided some time to practice applying the technique in different situations and experiment with what works. This method of self-discovery is usually a very powerful learning tool. This also encourages problem solving and goal orientation as opposed to only a skill base.

7. Learn from the lessons in the field. If a technique is never used in the field it's likely because the

officers realize that other methods are more desirable for obtaining their goals. Evaluate your program regularly to determine if changes need to be made. Pay attention to incident reports, court room testimony, and any surveillance video. If things are happening out there that you're not training for, change your program. This needs to be a constant evaluation process. Perhaps techniques not being used can be modified to better suit the unique environment your officers operate in.

8. Stop telling officers what they will and won't do. We are training adults. Adults in general, and especially law enforcement officers, will determine when and how to apply what they've learned. For this reason phrases like "Always do this..," or "Never do this..," are rarely appropriate. Encourage officers to think for themselves. You won't be in the field with them telling them when it's appropriate to make an exception to a generally accepted rule. It may be beneficial to explain to them where a particular response may fall in the scale of desirability and what the risks associated with the various responses are.

9. Include an "emotional triumph" lesson. If we're already teaching trainees how to survive a confrontation, why not teach them how to survive burnout, hyper vigilance, and the day-to-day stress of the job. More officers become victims of suicide and substance abuse then are killed in the line-of-duty each year. This is generally referred to as "emotional survival" but we've already explored why we need to move away from

that word. "Emotional triumph" or "emotional victory" may be more appropriate substitutes. This is an opportunity to educate officers about post traumatic stress, survival stress, stress management and post-retirement planning. There is excellent work available on the subject that trainers can implement into a 4 hour block and encourage their officers to follow up more on their own.

10. Change your PT program. Often trainers tell me the reason for their PT program is so that recruits will pass their exams at the end of training. While this is important is it really educating our officers? What happens once the recruit has completed training? If the change is made from PT to Phys Ed this puts an emphasis on teaching the officers how to maintain a healthy and active lifestyle for their entire career. Community resources can be researched and presented to the officers during training so that they know how to access programs after classes are completed. This also gives the trainers an opportunity to impress upon the recruits how critical performance related physical training and diet are.

11. Include an off duty lesson plan. Depending on your jurisdiction this lesson will change drastically. Department policy, municipal, state, and federal law must all be taken into account when preparing this lesson plan. Weapon choices may change drastically. If officers are permitted to arm themselves with a side arm off duty then it should be encouraged that the same, or similar, side arm as their on duty weapon be used. Officers must

be provided some direction as to what's expected when off duty and when not to get involved in an incident. If officers aren't permitted to be armed with a sidearm then edged weapons and/or martial arts weapons (i.e. cane and mini-stick) might be their only option. Recruits must be taught what's expected off duty and be encouraged to make good decisions. Family action planning can also be presented to the officers to help them in case of an off-duty incident.

12. Realize that you're teaching for the recruits, not for yourself. Our role as trainers is to provide our brother and sister officers with the skills and knowledge necessary to work safe, stay safe, and in return keep the public safe. Public safety is your primary focus. For this reason you must realize that most recruits are like sponges and want the trainer to answer every question for them. Instead encourage the officers to challenge what's being taught, think of creative alternatives, and answer questions for themselves. Constantly evaluate the program you deliver and your skills as a trainer, and don't be afraid to admit when you've discovered a more desirable way of doing things and encourage change. Your mission is a difficult and challenging one. When the public needs help they look to peace and police officers. When those officers need help they'll be looking to their trainers. As a trainer you may constantly find yourself in the situation where management and administration aren't supportive of your initiatives. Find ways to deliver the best program you can and constantly educate your administration until you have the support you need. Always remember

that it is your mission to educate your officers. You never know when the training you provided may influence someone's life. It may be the lesson you taught that saves an officer or the lesson you didn't teach that kills him/her/.

These 12 simple suggestions can help to modify any current defensive tactics program. Some of these suggestions may seem radical and unorthodox but I encourage you to ask yourself, is it time for a paradigm shift in my current DT program? If the answer is yes then I hope these suggestions find you and your officers well and provide the vehicle for positive change within your agency.

References: Although no specific material was referenced for this article I would like to thank several people for their influence and guidance that made this possible; LtCol. Dave Grossman, Dr. Alexis Artwohl, Dr. Bill Lewinski, Chuck Remsberg, Joe Truncale, Phil Messina, "Coach" Bob Lindsay, Dr. Gilmartin, Ken Murray, Hank Iverson, Orlando Mancina, Jay Creasey, and Brian Willis. I would highly recommend any material that these leaders in combat training produce. Although I've never even met some of you, your work and dedication has helped me to continually thirst for knowledge and empowers me to continually strive to be a better trainer tomorrow then I am today. Thank you.

Tom Gillis has been a martial artist for the last 13 years of his life. During that time he has studied many disciplines but has made Ninjutsu his passion and currently holds the rank of Shodan (black belt) in that system. He has been involved in Law Enforcement for the past 12 years and has been employed as an Alberta Sheriff for the last 5. During his career he has always been passionate about training and was instrumental in designing the Alberta Sheriffs' Control Tactics Program. In 2004 he started his own business, Foothills Training Services, that currently operates in Okotoks Alberta Canada. There he strives to provide the best quality training to both civilians and law enforcement. He can be reached at www.foothillstrainingservices.com or by email at foothillstraining@shaw.ca.

FORGING A WARRIORS METTLE

by Ron Borsch

A working definition of mettle for us here, will be the self-discipline of arousal to do ones best in the area of spirit, stamina and courage. Examples of warriors possessing extraordinary mettle were the Spartan's who in ancient Greece were known for great courage and fortitude. They practiced strict self-discipline and avoidance of comfort, luxury, and were undaunted by pain or danger. Spartan training methods, while most assuredly harsh, served them well.

In the modern world, except for third world countries, we are not likely to see such a "Spartan" existence model fully practiced. Creature comforts have grabbed hold, and we are likely to rely more on technology and "metal" as in hardware, rather than mettle as in intestinal fortitude, or pure "guts." Let us first discuss the term "warrior" and return later to the important subjects of spirit, stamina and courage.

Modern Warriors

There are many that deserve the title of warrior. Today, the first group that comes to mind is those in the military that defend our country. While not everyone in the military are genuine war-fighting warriors, we need to understand that those genuine war fighters on the "front line" cannot exist for long without support troops and logistics, and in today's world, that the "front-line" can suddenly be anywhere. In that respect, we can better understand the phrase, "All gave some, and some gave all."

The same might be said for our community's Safety Forces. Among our firefighters and police officers, there exist some genuine warrior protectors along with support troops. We do not always know who is which, or who will suddenly find himself challenged and embattled, especially in law enforcement.

There are also civilian warriors, whose hobby or recreation, involves honing their minds and bodies in some warrior fashion, such as contact type sports, hunting, etc. The focus of this essay will be upon the individual law enforcement warrior protector and different ways of forging a warrior's mettle, especially through warrior inoculations. Some inoculations, as we shall see, could require spirit, stamina, courage, or all three.

Small Dose Warrior Inoculations

One of the first to coin the term inoculation in connection with warrior training and preparation was psychologist Dave Grossman, Lt. Col. U.S. Army (Ret.). Grossman explains that a medical inoculation, as in the flu shot, is actually a little bit of the flu itself. The dose is small enough for our immune system to handle as it prepares itself to fight off the real thing. So, too, is how it would seem to work for stress, sight, sound, pain, etc.

Grossman speaks of "stress inoculations," especially during simulated gunfights. He has forwarded the concept of front-loading inoculations of stress and pain, as in simulations of gunfights using the painful sting of paint marking cartridges. These cartridges are fired with the officer's duty firearms after installing a safety adapter kit.

On his one time E-journal, Grossman fielded questions about various inoculations from officers all over America. The assorted ones the author recalls were typically from trainers and SWAT operators, about the possibilities of inoculating ourselves from horrible sights, sounds, etc. The author's questions were about inoculating ourselves against more serious pain than the mere momentary sting of marking cartridges. For example, the longer pain stimulus possible with the older contact-only-probes stun guns and TASERS.

Lets examine a couple mentor-model case histories, one planned and practiced for with inoculations over time, and the other, an off the scale surprise without the benefit of inoculation.

Modern Warrior Mentor Examples

Example one: Warrior enabler Richard Davis, (not a police officer), is a former Marine, and gunfight survivor. In his gunfight, Davis actually won against two armed robbers, but was shot by the third. The experience inspired him to invent soft body armor and he is the founder of Second-Chance Body Armor. Davis has walked the walk more than once, placing more than money where his mouth is. He has literally stood behind his product by shooting himself hundreds of times. This is a serious warrior, forging his mettle with serious training inoculations!

In one instance, Mr. Davis demonstrated (and documented on video), that an officer, wearing an appropriate vest, could be shot in the torso with a .44 Magnum, and have the wherewithal to "stay in the fight" engaging multiple adversaries, represented by bowling pins on a table. Mr. Davis did exactly that. Wearing a Second Chance Vest, he shot himself in the torso with a .44 Magnum revolver, turned and cleaned the bowling pins off of the table! While Mr. Davis's courage and moxie are not to be doubted, his demonstration was well planned, practiced and predictable, quite unlike the next example.

Example two: Los Angeles PD officer Stacy Lim was off duty returning home after a softball game. Not realizing a car full of gang-bangers was following her, she was exiting her vehicle in the driveway of her home. Several gang-bangers approached and the leader shot her in the chest with a .357 magnum, (the exit wound out of her back was the size of a tennis ball). First move and first blood, was claimed by the gang bangers, but Stacy's reaction was nothing short of amazing!

Stacy Lim stayed in the fight, shooting back on the move with her own pistol as she charged her retreating attacker, exchanging shots and getting hits with all four of her rounds. In the face of aggression from a real warrior, the remainder of the several gang-bangers fled, being "outnumbered" by Stacy. Their leader died, as did Stacy, (once in the ambulance, and twice on the operating table). Stacy struggled to live and is not only a gunfight winner, but also a survivor, going back to work at LAPD eight months after her shooting

Too Steep a Learning Curve!

Both Richard Davis and Stacy Lim are national treasures of the American law enforcement community. While the learning curves in their actions are too steep for most of us, we can learn much from their examples. Stacy has the right idea with her suggestion, **"YOU MUST PREPARE YOUR MIND FOR WHERE YOUR BODY MAY HAVE TO GO,"** and we should certainly listen to her. Her warrior performance was flawless, and surviving a heart-shot wound was miraculous. Her learning curve would be near impossible for many of us, especially if we had to start from square one. This is where we need to return to the small dose, warrior inoculation suggestions of Dave Grossman.

Start Early

Forging a warrior's mettle is best initiated in the early years of an officer's career when experience may be low, yet enthusiasm, dedication and physical fitness are at their highest levels. Physical fitness should be a balance of strength, endurance, (both muscular and aerobic/anaerobic), flexibility, agility and coordination. An early start can be the seed that could blossom for an entire career and beyond.

While physical fitness and health are certainly crucial keys in developing a warrior's mettle, many warrior protectors fail to develop more advanced and job related skills, especially mental and physical inoculation against unpleasant and distracting things that can fatally confront officers. Think about the sudden sensory overload in a surprise dangerous encounter. If it was you, and you had choices, would you choose to be confronted with a myriad of totally new-to-you experiences? Most of us, if we had the choice, would choose to plan, practice and prepare with reality-based simulation training to get these experiences beforehand.

In her book "Deadly Force Encounters," Dr. Alexis Artwohl identified several different phenomena that occur to us under stress: hyperventilation; accelerated heart rate; adrenaline rush; deteriorating cognitive process, loss of peripheral vision, (up to 70%); loss of depth perception; and loss of hearing.

The closest that we can get to receiving inoculations of these phenomena, is reality based simulations with both empty hand and firearm scenarios. The sooner this occurs in an officer's career, the better. This would be an example of forging a warrior's mettle. It would also be an example of intelligent design - front-loading specific experience into new officers rather than allowing haphazard experiences to occur randomly throughout an officer's career.

Innoculation Methods of Forging A Warrior's Mettle

Modern law enforcement's original "inoculation," was more unintentional than purposeful, with Chemical Mace©, and later OC/Pepper. In the early years with Chemical Mace©, few agencies required a training exposure. Law enforcement began to learn the hard way. Officers, in the middle of a violent encounter were surprised, (and even temporarily disabled), by their first dose of Chemical Mace© or OC by friendly fire. In time, most enlightened agencies began to require at least an indirect if not a full direct exposure.

The best training came from those agencies that required a direct exposure and some sort of fighting through the effects of the OC by a circuit of defensive and arrest motor skills which usually culminated in handcuffing.

The inoculation was designed to be enabling instead of disabling. This fighting through the effects is certainly an example of forging a warrior's mettle.

Listed below are examples of warrior spirit training aids which may be used to forge a warrior's mettle. The reader may have more ideas. Those listed, are from the author's personal experiences. Most are relatively accessible:

- Contact sports
- Martial Arts, (testing with punches to the solar plexus).
- OC Pepper or Chemical Mace
- Paint Ball, Marking cartridges, and Air-Soft plastic BB's
- Stun Gun
- With safety protocols: Firearms, to feel real percussion, muzzle blast, etc.
- With safety protocols: Distraction Devices, (Flash-Bang);
- TASER (M-26 & X-26).

Feel Muzzle Blast Now! Why Wait For Your First Gunfight?

The middle of your first gunfight is no time to experience sensory overload with new strange occurrences like feeling the hostile side of a firearm discharge, (minus the bullet of course). That is the reason for preparing now – with stress inoculation for these type incidents. The firearm percussion and flash-bang examples listed above were SWAT team experiences decades ago. These are not for everyone. They require multiple safety officers, and very close monitoring. Eye/ear protection is of course mandatory.

In years past, the safety protocol for the firearm-percussion exposure was a group of us sitting on the range floor, facing down-range, **(a wire or physical barrier was utilized to keep muzzles at least two to three feet above the tallest sitter).** Other team members rapidly discharged full-auto 9mm MP-5's and pump shotguns several feet behind and above us.

Similar to rappelling (which I will speak about later) there is an element of danger here. When safely and appropriately administered, the volunteer officers learn to confront the danger, conquer the stress, and trust their team mates, while gaining the bonus of an inoculation for muzzle blast and percussion.

Warrior or Whining-Weeping-Willows?

The street reality is that there are other factors involved with winning, survival and saving lives, especially when fatigued, wounded or injured. **Physical fitness alone may not be enough if officers shrink from reality based training that involves low level pain, discomfort, minor deprivations, and unpleasantness.**

Here is an example of an officer without an appropriate job-related stimulus: While the author was training the instructor staff at a large housing police department, the host commander, (formerly on the SWAT team of a large metropolitan PD), gave one of his best/worst example of "pain" avoidance. The commander related that one officer in a building where tear gas was deployed, jumped out of a second story window to avoid any slower method of retreating. Officers should have inoculations to prevent panic of this sort, where the resulting panic could cause far more serious injury than what was being avoided.

Spirit, Stamina and Courage

Let me address spirit, stamina and courage which I mentioned earlier in this article. "Spirit" would seem to be the easiest to practice. Spirit would have to start with a positive attitude and great outlook on life, developing into a dominating characteristic. "Courage," (having the nerve to be daring and brave), may be difficult to practice. We should think or it in terms of self-reliance skills that involve risk. One that comes to mind and is commonly used by many SWAT teams, is rappelling. Rappelling instructors or coaches can quickly detect any tentativeness in participants, and help them through this test, as a sort of rite of passage. Effective rappelling requires trusting yourself, your training, your instructor, teammates and your equipment.

"Stamina" requires work. Muscular and aerobic endurance are important. These can be worked on solo, with a partner, or a group and with or without equipment. Anaerobic endurance, as in sprints, and especially fighting skills, are part of a warrior's stamina. Both can be practiced solo. Training partners can make training easier, and in the case of combative motor skills, training partners, as in opponents, can be crucial.

The Warrior Countermeasure to a School Active Shooter

There was a time when a lone law enforcement shooter would think nothing of entering a school by himself on a report of a man with gun inside. It seems we went through a period of specialization requiring a SWAT team for the job. We woke up after Columbine, and started theorizing and began training with four man teams. The pendulum is starting to swing back toward the solo warrior protector officer, where we have documented successful aborting models.

The truth is, "Rapid response, early entry, and aggressive contact, by even a solo officer, has been, and is, the most effective countermeasure for mass-murder committed by the active shooter." Warriors should be forging their mettle and skills in anticipation of the opportunity to save lives. We need to instill a warrior protector model that says: "Not one more drop of innocent blood will occur on my watch, than I can possibly prevent"! At these times we are facing a rogue human punk that has chosen defenseless innocents as victims. All that is required is the right officer in the right place, early enough.

Conclusion

The officer warrior-protector knows not when he will be called upon for sudden, dangerous and maximal effort. From "A" for Ambush, to "Z" for the out of control "Zombie" created by drugs, insanity or both, the officers most prepared, not only survive, but win. Winning is the goal, survival is a lesser-included component of winning. It has been said that the will to win, pales in the face of the will to prepare to win. Preparation begins with the mind, but must evolve into forging the warrior's mettle.

In summation, forging a warrior's mettle, by necessity, starts with a foundation of good physical fitness, but must include a variety of warrior inoculations. Frequent and recent training in reality-based scenarios is good for stress inoculation. Forging a warrior's mettle should include inoculations of reality-based varieties of low level pain, discomfort, minor deprivations, and unpleasantness. These are best accomplished on a personal or voluntary basis. Meeting with like-minded warrior-protectors for group sessions can accelerate everyone's progress.

Throughout history, we have had positive role models such as the Spartan's. Later in history, we had examples such as the Samurai and Knights. America can lay claim to the Texas Rangers and their famous "One riot? One Ranger"! Modern law enforcement can look at the remarkable performance by LAPD's Stacy Lim. Now law enforcement officers should look inward and examine how they can best prepare and forge their own mettle.

PACT CONSULTANT GROUP
YOUR ONSITE RESOURCE FOR CONSULTING AND PRACTICAL ARREST CONTROL TRAINING
Serving area law enforcement psychomotor skill training needs since 1976

c/o Police Department, 165 Center Rd. Bedford Ohio 44146 (440) 232-7600 E-mail rbi0075@juno.com

After the Fight

"You gain strength, courage, and confidence by every experience in which you really stop to look fear in the face. You are able to say to yourself, "I have lived through this horror. I can take the next thing that comes along." You must do the thing you think you cannot do."

- Eleanor Roosevelt

THE ART OF ARTICULATION

by Brian Willis and Darren Leggatt

Every law enforcement trainer understands that simply doing what is right and using force that is reasonable and necessary, is not always enough. Officers must also be able to explain to an investigator, a judge, a jury or any court of enquiry that what they did at that moment in time was reasonable and necessary based on the totality of circumstances. It is my experience that in the majority of incidents where officers use force to control subjects, their actions are both reasonable and necessary. It is very common however for officers to struggle when they are asked to explain and justify their actions. In the past we would see them use generic statements in their documentation such as: "The subject resisted arrest and force was used to subdue him" When interviewed, they would use such eloquent explanations as: "He was an asshole." A quick review of the index in the law books fails to turn up the word asshole and it is not listed as a subject behavior category in any use of force models that I am aware of. In lethal force cases some officers simply state, "He had a knife." The mere fact the subject had a knife is again an insufficient explanation to justify a shooting. Another generic response in lethal force situations is "I feared for my life so I shot him." That fear is an important part of the big picture, but only a part.

Laura A. Zimmerman, Ph.D. of Klein Associates/ ARA made similar observations in her 2006 paper titled **Law Enforcement Decision Making During Critical Incidents: A Three-Pronged Approach to**

Understanding and Enhancing Law Enforcement Decision Processes. In that document she states:

> "After actual incidents, officers often justify their actions by claiming that the suspect was "aggressive" or "hostile" or that the suspect was "acting suspiciously" or making "furtive movements." These non-elaborative descriptions provide little justification for actions…"

A growing trend in North America is that officers lock into subject behavior categories on a use of force model to explain why they used a specific force response option. The officer states that the subject was assaultive and therefore he was justified in using a baton strike. While a baton may be a very reasonable option there is insufficient information in this explanation to justify it.

Administrators, trainers, and legal counsels around North America are looking for answers as to why this is happening. These answers are diverse and may vary dramatically depending on whom you ask. Some of the possible answers include:

1. Officers and agencies have become reliant on the technology such as in car video cameras, Tasercams®, etc which takes the story telling power from the officer and defers it to a tool.

2. The proliferation of police unions and associations and their leaders who encourage officers to say the absolute minimum.

3. The 'Hollywood Factor' that results in the current generation of police officer being subjected to a

cop show an hour, none of which reflect the reality of use of force events or of the profession.

4. The all too common question in training environments: "What category of subject can we use this with?"

The objective of this article is to provide some observations and present some thoughts and ideas on how we can begin to change this trend. We will begin by determining what we mean by articulation.

Articulation

When I talk about articulation I am referring to the ability to explain verbally, and in writing why the officer's actions were reasonable and necessary based on the totality of circumstances (the BIG picture).

Articulation (wordnet.princeton.edu/perl/webwn)
is defined as:

- give voice: put into words or an expression; expressing yourself easily or characterized by clear expressive language;
- express or state clearly
- articulated: consisting of segments held together by joints

The ability to express one's self easily and clearly using expressive language and to join all the elements of the event together is an art, rather than a science. It is the art of storytelling and it is this art that is often missing from articulation. Story telling has been used throughout history to pass along knowledge, wisdom and to share our experiences. Books, both fiction and non-fiction, employ the art of story telling. Movies and television use the power of multi media to bring stories to life. Parents read stories to their children and tell stories around the dinner table and the campfire to both educate and entertain their children.

Cops tell stories about calls and arrests in an easy to understand and free flowing manner all the time in the coffee shop, the lunchroom, or over a beer with their peers. Unfortunately, when they have to tell the same story in a report or on the witness stand their stories become brief, stilted, lacking emotion and expression, and filled with 'cop speak'. As a result they have a tendency to leave out important details that allow the interviewer, judge or jury to form a vivid image in their mind of what the officer was faced with at 3:00 A.M. in that dark alley. The officer often comes across sounding more like a robot than a human being who did his/her best when faced with a difficult and often rapidly evolving situation in which his/her safety and the safety and well being of others was at risk.

In his book A Whole New Mind: Why Right-Brainers Will Rule the Future Daniel H. Pink talks about the shift over time in which society has placed a greater emphasis on facts than stories. One of the concerns he has with this is that it runs contrary to how our minds actually work since we remember stories more than pure facts. He goes on to state "When facts become so widely available and instantly accessible, each one becomes less valuable. What begins to matter more is the ability to place these facts in context and to deliver them with emotional impact. And that is the essence of the aptitude of Story—context enriched by emotion."

Pink goes on to quote Don Norman Crissply from his book Thing That Make Us Smart:

"Stories have the felicitous capacity of capturing exactly those elements that formal decision methods leave out. Logic tries to generalize, to strip the decision making from the specific context to remove it from subjective emotions...Stories are important cognitive events, for they encapsulate, into one compact package, information, knowledge, context, and emotion."

This statement by Crissply identifies the art of articulation and the need for training officers in the art of story telling.

The search for answers as to why officers struggle in their ability to explain and justify their actions must lead us to a variety of locations - including the classroom, the training room, and the range. Most importantly however, it must lead us to look in the mirror. It is my contention that we need to more closely examine the way we teach use of force to determine where the disconnect exists between the officer's ability to act in a manner that is reasonable and necessary and the ability to articulate the reasonableness of his/her actions.

Use of Force – Continuums or Models

There is great debate in North America currently about whether or not we need to keep or abandon Use of Force Continuums. I have listened to people on both sides whom I respect and they all make valid points to support their position. Having listened to both sides I am not convinced that Use of Force Continuums are the sole cause for the inability of offices to articulate their actions as much as how they are taught. I strongly believe however, that we need to eliminate the word 'Continuum' and replace it with the word 'Model'. The rationale for this is that the word continuum suggests an incremental application of force rather than a level of force response that is reasonable and necessary based on the totality of circumstances. Model infers that this is a guideline or framework to help people understand what options an officer has available based on the totality of circumstances.

The Classroom

Classroom training in use of force needs to cover a variety of areas including:

- Legal authority to use force.
- Relevant case law decisions.
- Constitutional issues affecting use of force.
- Situational factors.
- Subject behaviors.
- Response options.
- Documentation.

I believe most agencies do a good job of teaching the legal and constitutional issues. The question that arises is whether these areas be taught as part of the overall use of force / officer safety package or in isolation as part of the 'academic studies'. Without putting this critical information in the context of the subject behaviors and situational factors officers face on the street the legal aspects are often confusing for the officers. When addressing subject behaviors the focus needs to be just that – behaviors (not behavior categories). Many recruits now entering the profession of law enforcement have little or no experience with interpersonal human aggression so they have no frame of reference when discussing subject behaviors.

It is important then to have classroom discussions about the types of behaviors that subjects may demonstrate and where possible to show them video footage of these behaviors. These behaviors must be taken in context so it is critical that an examination of the situational factors is built into these discussions. The classroom discussions can then move to the range of response options available to the officer when confronted with these behaviors. As training progresses and officers receive more training in additional force response options the discussions can expand to include these. Ideally these discussions would be followed up with video footage of officers successfully applying each of the force options discussed.

In order to allow new officers to understand that no tool or technique is 100% effective 100% of the time it is valuable to show video footage of officers using force response options that are reasonable and necessary but unsuccessful in gaining the subject's compliance. This creates opportunities for them to begin to imagine what they would do next to establish control by incorporating problems solving skills into the lessons.

Communications training needs to go beyond the realm of tactical communication. It is critical for officers to have skills in deflecting and defusing aggression and the ability to resolve conflicts in the field with verbal and non-verbal communication skills. Once the situation is resolved however they need skills in story telling to successfully navigate the reporting system and the legal system. Officers need the ability to make powerful presentations on the stand. Communication consultant Chez Lorincz says the three essential principles that allow a presenter to communicate effectively are:

1. Be yourself
2. Use clear thought
3. Use strong feeling

All of these principles can and should be taught to officers during use of force training and officers need to be rewarded in training when they communicate in this manner.

There have also been significant changes to law enforcement documentation over the years. As a profession we have moved away from officers writing their own reports and moved into the world of phoning in reports. Committing thoughts to paper by writing reports allowed for the details to come out and be expanded upon. In order to collect statistics many agencies have gone to check box Use of Force reports where there is no narrative. This type of report stifles the articulation abilities of the officer. Even the phone in data entry systems are created for the ease of the officer, perhaps not allowing the details of the events to be captured and explored to the level they should be.

The Training Room

The message from the classroom must be carried forward into the combatives training area. This is accomplished in a number of ways. First the officers must understand that the most important role they will ever perform in training is when they are playing the role of the subject. It is just that – a role they must play. They need to imagine they are the subject and display all the appropriate body language and verbiage to allow the officer to learn to read the situation and then quickly and appropriately respond to threat cues.

A question often asked in training rooms is "What category of subject can we use this technique/tool/tactic on?" This question is asked to reinforce the classroom theory and to make sure the officer can answer the question correctly on the use of force exam. The problem with this question is that it creates a direct link in the mind of the officer between the response option and the subject behavior category. When asked following an incident to explain why the officer selected that option his or her trained response becomes "because he was this category of subject." A better question in the training room would be "What subject behaviors and situational factors would allow us to use this option?" This question creates a link between totality of circumstances and options therefore training the officers to identify and articulate the big picture. A follow up question could be "Based on those factors what other options do you have available to you?" These types of open-ended questions take away the labels, tags and shortcuts resulting in a greater ability for the officer to speak to behaviors and options using common language.

In keeping with the themes from the classroom it is critical to build failure drills into all use of force training. This means that officers must be presented with situations in training where the technique or tool fails to gain control of the subject and the officer must transition to another response option. Officers should also be placed in situations where they have to transition from one response option to another due to the fact that the dynamics of the situation have changed. For example following the initial baton strike an officer may end up too close to the subject to use the baton for additional strikes and it would be more desirable to use knee strikes or some other form of empty hand control.

Additionally, the messages taught in the classroom and the control tactics training room must be the same as those delivered during firearms training, vehicle stop training, building clearing training, and rapid intervention training. To this end, it is important that instructors within these fields are cross trained or at least know definitively what is taught in each area of expertise.

Debriefings

Training debriefings following scenarios or similar exercises are a great opportunity to learn from the experience, determine what we would do differently in similar incidents in the future, and practice the skill of articulation. Unfortunately however, we are often so eager to get into discussions surrounding tactics that we gloss over the explanation surrounding the use of force. As a result, officers are allowed to use generic statements and simply refer to subject behavior categories from the model so the instructor can mark those off on the check sheet and move onto the 'meat' of the debrief. By doing this, officers are being trained and conditioned that this is an acceptable way to explain their actions.

Instructors must take the time to conduct comprehensive debriefings in order to maximize all the learning opportunities. Failing to do so is a disservice to the officer and the agency. In order to conduct full and effective debriefings however, the instructors running the scenarios must have an in depth understanding of the totality of use of force authority and articulation. They must also be familiar with what has been taught in the classroom and the training room to avoid any conflicting messages.

It is worth noting in relation to debriefings (and investigations) that one of the potential flaws in the way we examine use of force in the aftermath is that many people believe the decision made by the officer at the time is based on examining all the options available to them, precluding options that would not work and selecting the best option. Gary Klein in his book Sources of Power: How People Make Decisions talks about his research into recognition primed decision-making. Klein and his associates found that in circumstances similar to what officers face in the street they do not examine a range of options. They use a singular evaluation approach whereby they identify one option that will suffice to solve the problem. Klein refers to the decision-making strategy Herbert Simon (Nobel Prize winner in Economics) referred to as satisficing: selecting the first option that works. Satisficing is more efficient than optimizing - especially in situations where there is greater time pressure, dynamic conditions and ill-defined goals, which refers to trying to come up with the best strategy.

Simulators / Videos

Many agencies are now utilizing some form of simulator technology in their training. This ranges from interactive judgmental use of force simulators to driving simulators. A use of force simulator provides a few unique opportunities to trainers. Prior to going through a complete scenario on the simulator a recruit class could be divided into two groups. Each group is brought in and shown a scenario up to the point where the officer would use force to control the subject. At this point they could be given some time to imagine in their mind what control option they would utilize to control the subject. The recruits are then sent out to independently make notes of the incident while the second group is brought in and shown a different scenario. They go through the same process of imagining their control option and making notes.

The two groups are then brought back together, paired up and each explains their scenario and response to their partner. Once both groups have had a chance to tell their story they watch the two scenarios again to see how close their explanation was to what actually occurred. This could be repeated as often as the instructors desire – in order to develop the officer's skills in observation, note taking and articulation. The timing of the explanation and the review of the videos can vary. In some cases the entire process would take place immediately after they have finished making their notes. In other cases the explanation could be done immediately following the note taking and then 24 to 72 hours later the officer would retell the story and watch the video to see what effect time has on the officers recollection of the event.

It is not necessary to have a simulator to conduct these types of exercises. If the agency does not have simulators or does not wish to use their scenarios in this manner the same process can be used with video clips of incidents. Most trainers have a large library of video clips they can use and if not the videos are available from a variety of sources. The ideal method of using these clips would be to project the scenarios onto a large screen by running the video through an LCD projector. This provides the officers with a closer to real life view of the incident and makes it easier for them to imagine being there. If this is not possible the video can be shown on a television.

Trainers can also become creative and utilize cameras to shoot videos of different subject behaviors and actions which could be used at specific times in their programs. It is not necessary to have hi-tech video equipment to complete this task. The purpose of the video is to expose officers to subject behaviors and allow them to begin to learn to observe, respond, document and then tell the story. Actors from the local college, family members or plain clothes personnel can play the roles of the subjects in these videos. If these people are utilized it is important to ensure they understand the behaviors that are necessary for the video segment.

Similar articulation exercises could be utilized with driving simulators in which the officer is involved in a pursuit followed by note taking and articulation exercises. For agencies utilizing both driving and use of force simulators it is beneficial to have them at the same location so the officer can transition from the driving simulator to a use of force incident.

The Challenge

The challenge then to all use of force instructors is to find better ways in which we can not only enhance the decision making skills of officers but also to put the 'art' into articulation. It is not enough to make good decisions, the officer must also be able to explain in common language why, given the totality of circumstances, the decisions they made and the actions taken were reasonable and necessary for them.

Brian Willis is an internationally recognized professional trainer and speaker. Brian draws on his 25 years of law enforcement experience as a member of the Calgary Police Service and 19 years of training experience to provide cutting edge training to law enforcement officers and trainers throughout North America. In 2005 Brian was honored with a Lifetime Achievement Award in recognition of his contributions to officer safety training in Canada.

Brian is the president of Winning Mind Training, editor of the highly acclaimed book W.I.N.: Critical Issues in Training and Leading Warriors and a contributing writer for the book Warriors: On Living With Courage, Discipline and Honor (www.warriorspiritbooks.com). He is also a principle for Warrior Spirit Books (www.warriorspiritbooks.com) and the functional strength and fitness company Kick Ass Conditioning (www.kickassconditioning.com).

Brian serves as an Advisory Board member for the International Law Enforcement Educators and Trainers Association (ILEETA), ForceOneReadiness.com, and served as a member of the National Advisory Board for Police Marksman Magazine from 2000 to 2007. He is a member of NTOA, ITOA, IALEFI, National Guild of Hypnotists and the Canadian Association of Professional Speakers. He is the Editor of the ILEETA Review and writes a regular column for the ILEETA Use of Force Journal. Brian can be reached through his website at www.winningmindtraining.com.

Darren Leggatt is an 18 year veteran law enforcement officer with a major Canadian police agency. He is currently the Sergeant in charge of the development and delivery of Officer Safety, Subject Control Tactics,

Emergency Vehicle Operations, Incident Command, Use of Force and Communications training for his agency of over 1600 sworn officers.

Darren's career has been mostly operational in nature, spending over 8 years as a police dog handler and trainer, with an expertise in high risk tactics and explosive detection. He has planned operational tactics for explosive detection and sanitization surrounding 9-11, The G8 Summit, and the Royal Visit 2005. Darren has also served as a Search and Rescue Management Specialist for his agency for over 10 years, coordinating numerous urban based search and rescue operations.

Darren has various instructor level certifications in subject control techniques, less lethal munitions, chemical munitions, vehicle operations, and officer safety tactics.

INCOMPLETE OFFICER SURVIVAL: THE IMPORTANCE OF SELF-AID TRAINING

by Eric Dickinson

"The fate of the wounded rests in the hands of the ones who apply the first dressing."

- Nicholas Senn, M.D.

One of the most important duties of anyone who leads and trains warriors is the ability to evaluate current training and identify areas where additional emphasis is required. Few if any law enforcement officers have all the training they should have. With so little time and money, many responsibilities and constantly changing laws, policies, equipment and training methods, it's a wonder that officers are able to conduct their duties with any reasonable level of effectiveness. The fact that they persevere and perform their duties in such a professional manner is a testament to the men and women who make up the ranks of the estimated 900,000 officers, deputies, troopers and agents across the United States.

The 1970s were the deadliest decade in American law enforcement history with an average of 228 officers killed in the line of duty each year. In response to those deaths, numerous advances occurred that increased the safety of officers on the street. The development of body armor and the advent of the officer survival training movement have undoubtedly led to the reduction of officer deaths over the last 30 years. Despite advances in training related to firearms, defensive tactics, intermediate weapons, calming techniques and mental preparation, one critical area of officer survival training has gone largely ignored. That issue is self applied medical aid.

Are We Failing Our Officers?

"Do not expect the combat fairy to come bonk you with the combat wand and suddenly make you capable of doing things that you never rehearsed before."

- Lt. Col. Dave Grossman, On Combat

According to the National Law Enforcement Officers Memorial Fund (NLEOMF), 181 law enforcement officers were killed in the United States in 2007 for the highest number of line of duty deaths since the 1970s. Thirty-eight percent of those officers were killed by gunfire and 46% died in traffic related accidents. Based on prior year data from the FBI, an estimated 15,000+ officers will have been injured in assaults during the same time period. No statistics could be found stating how many officers were simply injured through accidental means during the same period.

Without knowing intimate details of each incident and the sustained injuries, we will never know how many deceased or injured officers may have been in a position to save their own lives or mitigate their injuries by treating themselves initially. However, the advent of in-car video cameras has given us visual record of incidents where improved first aid and/or self-aid could have benefited injured officers. Some of those officers who were injured and did not apply self-aid are with us today primarily due to a significant amount of luck. It is not my desire to second guess or criticize those officers as they most likely did whatever they had been trained to do. If any fault should be assigned, it is my belief that fault lies with US, the instructors, supervisors and administrators. We are responsible for preparing our officers to win and survive violent encounters and this topic is the source of numerous books, articles and training courses. At the same time, we cannot overlook the fact that officers may also be injured in non-violent situations such as single vehicle car accidents, falls and negligent discharges of firearms. Are your officers capable of providing self aid until further help arrives?

Your officers probably received some type of first aid training during their basic academy. Are they required to refresh those skills on a regular basis? Even if they have regular first aid training, have they ever considered the possibility of treating themselves? If you are familiar with Lt. Col. Grossman's books or lectures you have probably already heard or read his quote above. If you haven't trained your officers in self-aid, how can you expect them to perform self-aid under stress? First aid on someone else is an entirely different animal than treating oneself. Seeing their own blood and torn tissue and feeling the associated pain is something that officers must be prepared for.

Still not convinced that your officers need self-aid training? Consider that many officers in the U.S. perform their duties alone in solo patrol units and often in small departments in rural areas resulting in lengthy response times for back-up officers and EMS and often longer transport times from the scene of their injury to an appropriate hospital. Even officers in large metro areas can find themselves terribly alone in the middle of a city full of people as they wait for help that is stuck in traffic or overstressed with calls for service. Considering that an officer with a severed femoral artery can bleed to death within a few minutes, every second that passes without medical intervention puts an officer closer to death. Every red blood cell counts. Each one contains life in the form of oxygen, nutrients and warmth for the body. Don't waste them. The greatest EMS personnel and hospitals in the world can't save you if you don't leave them something to work with.

Know Your Needs and Capabilities

"Do what you can, with what you have, where you are."

- Theodore Roosevelt

The post-9/11 world and subsequent War on Terror has led to the first truly remarkable advancements in combat medical care since the use of helicopter transport for wounded soldiers became common during the Korean War. Blood clotting agents, combat tourniquets, improved pressure dressings and numerous other products and treatment methods have been rapidly developed and deployed along with troops in combat.

Many would agree that the lines between law enforcement and the military have blurred somewhat in recent years, usually for the betterment of both. While military operations have increasingly required "less-lethal" capabilities and lower collateral damage, law enforcement has seen a need for improved weapons, armor and tactics to respond to domestic terrorism such as the North Hollywood shootout and the Columbine and Virginia Tech massacres, not to mention the increasing threat of international terrorism.

Unfortunately, some of the medical training and products developed for military combat operations has recently been directed at and marketed to law enforcement with little understanding or acknowledgment of the differences between civilian medical care in the continental U.S. and military medical operations under combat conditions overseas. We have and continue to learn much from the medical lessons learned during combat but those lessons must be carefully evaluated as to their applicability to domestic law enforcement. With a few exceptions, typical injuries and patient evacuation times that are common to combat zones are drastically different than those commonly encountered in the civilian world where medical response capability is typically faster and more dependable. Additionally, states have varying requirements and regulations in which some of these treatments can be administered. A soldier with 40-60 hours of medical training may be allowed to perform medical procedures in a combat zone that only a paramedic or higher with over 1000 hours of training is allowed to perform domestically.

So what do we need to do to prepare our officers to treat their own injuries? Focus your training on the very basics of first aid. When addressing bleeding control, focus on direct pressure, elevation, pressure points and tourniquets. Consider whether or not your officers have the ability to carry medical supplies on their person. Most patrol officers don't have a great deal of load bearing capability that is not taken up by all their other gear. Even if they are able to carry supplies on-duty, what will they do if injured during an off-duty encounter when they don't have their supplies? What will they do if they apply a fancy combat pressure dressing and then observe they are bleeding through it?

All officers need to be taught ways to improvise their self-care utilizing whatever items are at hand. A ticket book, clothing or a bare hand can be a substitute for an improvised dressing when direct pressure is needed. Clothing, belts, plastic tie restraints and shoelaces have all been used as improvised tourniquets and a baton or pistol magazine can be used as a windlass. A plastic baggie or latex glove can be used to create an improvised occlusive dressing to treat a sucking chest wound. Teach your officers to obey Clint Eastwood's words from the movie "Heartbreak Ridge" and Improvise, Adapt and Overcome. Teach your officers to recognize the problem (injury) and base their treatment on whatever items they have available for use.

If your officers are fortunate enough to be able to carry one or more of the new combat tourniquets, clotting agents or pressure dressings, ensure those officers are being adequately trained with them. If you distribute these products to your officers without training, you will simply compound their problems. Their improper use of a product could result in the officers losing their lives instead of saving them. Adding laser sights to a poor shooter's pistol will not solve a basic marksmanship problem regarding the use of iron sights. Giving your officers expensive medical supplies without a basic understanding of self applied medical care with improvised materials will do the same thing. We want to SOLVE a training problem, not simply add another training problem on top of the first.

It Won't Happen to Me

Every time a news crew points a camera at the scene of a workplace or school shooting, they always record a quote from a witness or neighbor who states, "I never thought it could happen here." Brian McKenna, retired police sergeant and longtime writer of the "Officer Down" column for Police Marksman and Law Officer magazines, has said that all but one of the officers he interviewed over the last 20 years stated that they did not think they were about to get into a shooting. Too many officers have found themselves victim of this dangerous line of thinking whether they find themselves in a shooting or just a scuffle during handcuffing. They go to work each day and tell themselves, "It won't happen to me." This problem seems to be magnified in small, rural departments where complacency can often prove to be an officer's worst enemy. Understand that it CAN happen to your officers and their self-aid training may be the only reasonable chance they have for survival.

For those officers who still refuse to acknowledge that they could be shot or cut, remind them how many officers are killed or injured each year due to traffic accidents. An officer struck by a passing car in an isolated area may have to begin self-care techniques just the same as an officer injured by felonious assault. I will pose this question again, how long can your officers realistically expect to wait for EMS response and transport? How much life are they willing to lose during that wait?

Whenever I propose improved first aid training for law enforcement, I hear the inevitable comments from a few officers that they went into law enforcement and would have gone into EMS if they wanted to perform first aid. By focusing first aid training on self-aid techniques, you personalize the issue and may sell even the least enthusiastic officers in your department on the importance of this training. They may even show an interest in training they have not demonstrated for many years. Though the training is focused on self-aid, the fundamentals of emergency care are the same regardless whom the patient is and officers will leave the training better armed to care for an injured colleague or civilian in addition to himself or herself.

The Trainer's Challenge

"No officer should be injured or killed because of something I taught them or FAILED to teach them."

- Arlen Ciechanowski, Assistant Director, Iowa Law Enforcement Academy

For the last several years, there has been a subtle debate among some law enforcement instructors over semantics. Should officers be taught to utilize a "winning mindset" or a "survival mindset"? Without resurrecting the whole debate here, I must point out that it does little good to win the fight with a violent offender if an injured officer sits patiently and allows him or herself to bleed to death while waiting for emergency medical services to arrive. Officers must be taught to understand that while the fight may be over, their work is not.

How do we train for this? Scenario based training has been well utilized in recent years with other topics and works to a reasonable extent with self-aid. By using fake injuries and blood, known as moulage, and applying them to student-officers, you can begin to desensitize them to the sight of their own blood and devastating injuries. The required set up time and lack of associated pain will probably prevent this from being the most ideal simulation but it can make for an effective isolation exercise. If you don't have the time and resources to use moulage, at least have officers perform self-aid techniques in the dark or without the effective use of both hands. For truly stressful first aid simulations, make up the student-officer's regular partner with moulage injuries and theatrical blood and send the student-officer into a simulated "officer down" call. The sight and sounds associated with a seriously injured and recognized co-worker would provide a valuable test of the officer's ability to focus on critical lifesaving techniques.

As a law enforcement officer you have a responsibility to those who can't protect themselves. As a law enforcement leader and trainer, you have an even greater responsibility to the protectors themselves. Teach them to win the fight. Teach them to survive the aftermath by performing proactive self-aid. Teach them to live to protect another day.

Eric Dickinson is a Senior Police Officer with the Vinton (Iowa) Police Department. He is an EMT-Intermediate (85) and state certified EMS instructor and evaluator. He also teaches several topic areas related to police use of force and officer survival including firearms, defensive tactics and intermediate weapons. He is an Eagle Scout and credits his years as a youth and adult leader in the Boy Scouts of America for inspiring him to go into law enforcement and EMS and to lead and train others. First Aid was the first merit badge he earned as a Scout.

He holds a BS in Public Administration and an AA in Law Enforcement. He is an adjunct instructor at Hawkeye Community College (Waterloo, Iowa) and at Kirkwood Community College (Cedar Rapids, Iowa). He has presented training at regional and national conferences and has written articles that have been published in various professional trade publications including *Law Officer* magazine, the *Journal of EMS* (JEMS) and The *Firearms Instructor*. He is a member of ILEETA, IALEFI, NTOA, the Iowa EMS Association (IEMSA) and a life member of the National Eagle Scout Association (NESA). Eric can be contacted at edickinson49@hotmail.com.

ENEMY AT THE GATE

by Martin Smith

Helping to Understand and Cope Effectively With Stress and Anxiety

Understanding the Gate

The title of this article and the presentation it is drawn from is about becoming aware of the last and strongest defence we have, which is situated in the mind. The gate is a metaphor I use for the filter between the objective reality of the world and the internal processes of our mind, it is an essential part of our personal safety armoury and it can be our greatest ally, but all too often our greatest enemy.

How we perceive things and process them within us is crucial to our overall wellbeing. How we open the gate and what we allow our perceptions of the external World to affect us are down to us, we can choose how we feel and the internal state we operate from. I have been trained in the solution focused therapy approach known as the Human Givens and it is from this approach that I draw some of my understanding and methodologies for effective resolution to the issue of personal trauma and anxieties.

Through additional study in NLP, Hypnosis and general psychology I have sort to find effective ways to allow people to move on from the trap of anxiety disorders such as PTSD. The focus is on defending the gate and showing people that it is not a sign of weakness to suffer such conditions, nor is it a given that we must suffer such conditions for the rest of our lives. I have specialised in the treatment of anxiety disorders in my private practice and have seen first hand how these conditions can do far greater damage than any bullet, knife or physical injury. It is vital for every one in and around law enforcement to realise that these conditions can be tackled and effective and long lasting solutions attained, often without years of long and painful sole searching and treatment.

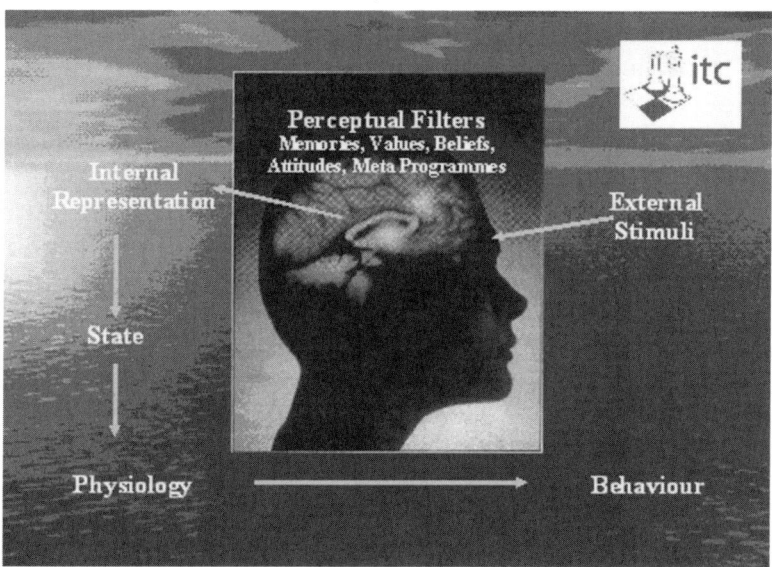

Understanding Human Needs

The Human Givens approach is a holistic therapeutic approach based on firm scientific understandings of how our mind/body system works and draws on the positive human resources we all have within us to fulfil the needs we all require. The needs are basic templates within us and seek fulfilment from the world around us. These needs are known as the Human Givens and include our need for safety, self esteem, control, autonomy, to name but a few. The Human Givens work from the understanding that we all have the resources inside us to enable us to fulfil our potential and so when we suffer emotional, psychological or physical trauma we all have the capability to move on from it and continue with a positive and healthy life. The problem comes in how to do this after a severe and difficult event when our whole system may be shouting to give up or retreat and hide.

Just because I believe we all have the resources within us to achieve great and positive outcomes, it does not follow that we know how to access such resources. This is often where many psychotherapeutic approaches fall down. If the client does not know how to access the resources then the therapist needs to show them and tell them how to. This can often break one of the old cardinal rules of therapy, which is not to give advice. The problem with this is, if the client does not know what to do, no amount of introspection and personal reflection is going to help.

I often use the analogy of the noise in the car engine. If you have noise in your car you could try and find it, and perhaps try and fix it. You could spend a great deal of time and energy on the problem and never find the answer, why, because if you do not know what you are looking for you are literally stumbling in the dark. For a person with PTSD or an anxiety disorder this can only compound the problem. If, however you took your car to a mechanic they may be able to point you in the right direction. You should still fix the problem but at least by seeking advice you can get a good idea about how to go about sorting the problem. This approach often gets strong, burly men past the idea that seeing a therapist is a sign of weakness and only something a wimp would do.

The Last Strong Hold and Ultimate Safe Guard

Many of us who train and manage officer safety training will often agree that we could always do more. That training is often seen as less of a priority and one that is the first to go when budget cuts are necessary. At the same time it is perhaps true to say that the quality of officer safety training is improving and developing all the time, and is better now than it has ever been. We now have training to develop the officer's mind and body before any incident. We have programmes which develop the officer's response to various encounters and levels of force, ways to handle stress in a variety of situations and even post incident training to deal with court and internal affairs investigations.

As a serving Police Officer for over twenty years, a great deal of which has been involved in officer safety training and development, I have always been a keen advocate of anything which will help anyone involved in law enforcement to stay safe. Nearly ten years ago I qualified as a psychotherapist and along side my work as a police officer I commenced private practice as a therapist. From there I began further study and work towards a doctorate in psychology with particular focus on post incident trauma. Over the past few years I have seen numerous people who have suffered psychological trauma and seen how it can impact on their lives. I have also been intrigued about how effectively we can treat such conditions and how often we do a lot of things which actually make trauma worse.

It also occurred to me having taught stress management to many officers just how much we tend to avoid people who are suffering any psychological complaint. The fear is often that if we try and help, try and talk to them we may send them over the edge. The question then sprung to mind about the type of training we do and how often it may be possible in a training session to trigger past trauma in a person. The issue here is not to say, stop doing any training that may trigger such responses, but rather to have some insight into what is happening to a person who is suffering and then have some ideas on how to help them rather than make it worse or even just ignore them.

This programme is not just about helping participants in your training sessions it is hopefully an insight into psychological trauma that can assist you with friends and colleagues who may be suffering or even yourself. The bottom line is that no matter how well trained we are and how well prepared we are, we may still fall at an incident. Yes the most important thing is to survive the encounter, but the focus here is then to move on after the event. It is not to just continue surviving long after the incident, but to be able to put the emotional trauma to one side and move on with life. Many have faced the worse case scenario and yet survived; the problem is that for some that is all they are still doing, surviving. Despite all they have been through the mind has a way of sometimes keeping us locked in past events that continually drive us down and keeping us locked in the past event. As trainers you will have people in your class or close friends or even yourself who are suffering in this way and for whom help is needed and guidance in breaking the cycle of negative emotion and trauma.

Teaching the physical skills and developing confidence is one aspect of training, but coping with the potential psychological damage in people is quite another. I am not suggesting we should all become psychologists or counsellors of troubled souls, but there are some simple things we can do which can help the situation rather than make things worse.

Tackling the Problem and What We Do Wrong

People are well meaning when they tell someone how bad it must have been to have been attacked or to have been in that particular incident, and how bad the person must be feeling about it. Other favourites I often hear are, "It's not your fault, don't blame yourself" or "You really could not have done anything about it, you did your best" all well meaning, but they do nothing to really help. The problem with a physical attack and especially one where an officer has been unable to help others in need at the time strikes at the very core of our self esteem and need for security and control. Words of sympathy and often just active listening with no real focus on how to move on do not help to breakdown the emotional turmoil someone can feel inside.

A favourite method of dealing with such issues is to get the person to talk about it. Two key problems occur with this, the first is that it can be very intrusive and sometimes, even though not intentional, quite judgemental. That aside the real problem in just going over past events is that by doing so we run those events again and again and in doing so reinforce the event and the patterns they generate in the mind. From these patterns come the very powerful emotional responses and then thoughts of being a failure or being violated and so the cycle of despair and negativity continue. It is important to remember how our memory works, each time we go over an event our brain has to reconstruct the event and so reinforce the pathways that in turn can keep the trauma alive.

This is not to say that talking through an event is wrong, it is how it is done. The reason talking should be to look at ways to break negative patterns, install new patterns and enhance the individual's feelings of worth and positive resources. Developing their current internal state to a point where they know they can come through and feel stronger and better. Constantly dwelling on the event and more importantly the negative internal state that goes with it does nothing to move the person on. The aim of the individual and those around them, including their instructor is to help focus on the resources they have inside them and utilise those resources to get positive results. During my research into effective treatment for anxiety and PTSD one approach that consistently came up was for an individual to talk to close friends and colleagues in a positive and supportive way.

The Positive Resources are Always There

A question I get asked so often by clients and students alike is that they just do not believe they have the capability at times to pull out of their negative state. If it is another person they are trying to help, they often say that they cannot find a way to access the positive resources. In the first instance the answer to this is very simple. If you think of a time in the past when you felt positive and resourceful, no matter when it was or what it was, if you can access such an event, and no matter how small or insignificant the event may have seemed at the time most people can find one. At this point you have already got that positive resourceful state installed and with practice of some simple techniques it is very possible to enhance and cultivate these past resources. If someone says that no matter how hard they try they still cannot access a positive state then we can utilise one of our most powerful and effective tools, the power of imagination.

If you cannot get the person to access a real state then get them to imagine what such a state would be like. By doing this we ignite the same neural pathways in the mind that would be activated if the event were real, and in so doing we change our internal state and thereby begin to break the cycle of negativity. Remember the law of reverse effect which states if you pitch will power against imagination, imagination will win out. As we imagine or remember a positive resource we then run the emotional and physical state in the here and now and so immediately begin to move ourselves or others we are helping, forward and out of the potential depth of despair and negativity.

A simple example of this is to try and resist your favourite piece of food, place the item in front of you, especially when you are really hungry and then try to resist eating it. No doubt you can but how hard is it to do so. Now look at that favourite, delicious item of food and then begin to imagine that it has been standing for a few days, imagine it has been prepared by someone who has a really bad cold and they have been coughing all over it, then imagine that same person has not had a bath for a month and just been to the toilet. Do you begin to get the picture, does that item start to become far less attractive.

The use of positive imagination cannot be over emphasised when dealing with powerful negative feelings. Another thing to note is how people describe past traumas to you, if they are generally ok about the event they will describe it in the past tense and be what we call disassociated from the event. That means that they are not there living it NOW, which is what someone who is traumatised will be doing. They will talk in present tense about how they are feeling rather than how they did feel. In trauma situations the person returns to the event and relives it over and over again. A key way to break this cycle is to get them thinking about it in past terms and as though they are a neutral observer. Short exercises in the Enemy at the Gate presentation highlight how easily these things can be done.

Effectively psychological trauma is one off learning that has been burnt deep into the emotional centres of the brain so that every time the event is recounted it immediately stimulates intense emotional feelings which often the individual cannot control or at least feel like they can control. Through a number of key processes it is possible to start to move that person away from the strong emotional state and in to a more rational and cognitive thinking process which allows them to feel they have control of the event. As stressed earlier in this article the aim is not to be a therapist, but as instructors just to gain a better understanding to what is happening to a person and at least apply some initial "psychological first aid" as I often term it prior to them seeking more professional help.

If you were teaching a class and someone received a physical injury you would assist them prior to getting more experienced medical help, what we are trying to do here is give some vital support to people who are also suffering although the injury is perhaps not quite so easy to spot.

Martin J. Smith PhD is a Police Inspector with Nottinghamshire Police. He has over twenty years policing experience and is currently the Force's Professional Development Manager overseeing the training of core operational policing skills

A qualified trainer and assessor of competency based training programmes, Martin presents to a variety of Public and Private Organisations both in the UK and in the United States of America, designing and writing training programmes as well as individual personal development programmes and personal coaching strategies.

Martin is the Lead Trainer for Nottinghamshire Police in Officer Safety Training as well as being a qualified Public Order trainer and tactical advisor. He is a hostage negotiator for the Force.

He is a regular writer for a number of UK Magazines and has designed and taught a number of personal safety and conflict management packages to various private and public sector groups. He is a fellow of **The Human Givens Institute** where he holds a diploma in psychotherapy working from Solution focused and Brief therapy methods drawn from the Human Givens approach. He has a Bachelors degree in psychotherapy with specific focus on clinical hypnosis and a Doctorate in Psychology.

He is a member of the prestigious **International Law Enforcement Educators and Trainers Association**

- **ILEETA** and **The American Women's Self Defence Association – AWSDA** and is an executive board member for AWSDA. He attends numerous conferences in the United States and presents on a number of subjects. Martin has recently been presenting his **Enemy at the Gate Programme** to numerous Organisations and Law Enforcement Agencies.

You can contact Martin direct on **07973 410010** or email him at mjsitc@aol.com
Or visit his website at www.taking-control.co.uk

OFFICER TRAINING: DEFENDING YOUR ACTIONS IN CIVIL RIGHTS LITIGATION

by Laura L. Scarry

Today's law enforcement officer is better equipped than ever to "win" physical encounters on the street. This is due, in part, to the availability of the latest technological advances in police equipment, and better training on the different methods to defeat combative suspects. Despite the advances in law enforcement, a recent press release by the National Law Enforcement Officers Memorial Fund demonstrates that with the exception of 2001 (when many police officers were killed during the terrorist attack of September 11), 2007 was the deadliest year for police officers in nearly two decades. The report also shows that there was a 33% increase in the number of police officers facing death by gunfire from 2006 to 2007.

While it is difficult to determine the cause for the increase in violent deaths to officers, or to establish a practical solution to curb violence against law enforcement personnel, police officers undoubtedly will be trained to be ever more vigilant when it comes to officer safety in performing their day-to-day duties. It only makes sense.

Unfortunately, not only are officers facing an increase of deadly force confrontations on the street, they are also more likely than ever, for whatever reason(s), to be the faced with civil rights lawsuits as a result of performing legitimate law enforcement tasks. However, it appears that with all the training that police officers undergo to protect themselves on the street, it is woefully inadequate when it comes to "winning the battle" against accusations of wrongdoing in civil litigation.

As a former police officer, I usually testified in court as a witness called by the city prosecutor or county state's attorney for a traffic violation, misdemeanor arrest or, on the very rare occasion, a felony arrest. On those occurrences, I appeared in advance of the hearings to discuss the facts of each case with the attorney over the course of a few minutes. Now, this is not a criticism of the government attorneys I worked with; however, rarely was I given any direction as to what role my testimony played or the manner in which I should testify. Any guidance usually amounted to, "what ever you do, keep your answers short and to the point, and don't volunteer any information."

It was a little frustrating testifying under those circumstances because I felt that I was being kept in the dark. But, it was something that I eventually learned to accept. After all, I was only a witness on behalf of the prosecution. As a witness, I didn't have much at stake in testifying. Sure, I wanted the prosecution to obtain a conviction. Indeed, a conviction would give me justification for doing my job or, in other words, catching the bad guys. However, if the prosecution failed to get the conviction, I also learned with time that other things might have played a role in the prosecution's failure to get the conviction. Frankly, it was no sweat off my back; maybe the next prosecution of one of my arrests would be successful.

It's a little bit different, though, when the officer is personally named as a defendant in a civil rights lawsuit. In that case, the officer's own conduct is called into question. Undoubtedly, a lot more is at stake: the legitimacy of the arrest, the officer's reputation, his credibility, and possibly his future as a law enforcement officer. Further, in the extreme situation, the officer's assets may be at risk if the plaintiff is suing the officer for punitive damages. In other words, it is personal.

But, with proper preparation or training, an officer will fare much better in presenting testimony either in his deposition or at trial. Of course, this process entails much more than reviewing police reports and records. Certainly, the most important aspect of being prepared to provide testimony in civil litigation is understanding three separate but related components: the defense theory, the role of the questioning attorney, and the role of the accused—or in this case—the officer.

First, a police officer that is sued civilly should understand the theory of the defense. This necessarily implies that the officer understands the claims alleged against him. Is he being sued for false arrest? Excessive force? Malicious prosecution? Once he understands the nature of the claims, including the elements necessary to make each claim, he can appreciate the defense theory.

Usually the defense theory centers on the plaintiff's failure to prove one of the elements of the claim against the officer. For example, in a false arrest claim, one of the elements that a plaintiff generally must prove is that the police officer lacked probable cause to make the arrest. On the other hand, the typical defense theory is that the officer had sufficient probable cause to make the arrest. Thus, the officer should expect the defense attorney to remind him that his testimony should reiterate all of the circumstances surrounding the arrest. Of course, this is not to suggest that the officer should respond to questions with "I had probable cause" over and over in his testimony. Instead, the officer should explain the facts that led him to believe that he had probable cause to take whatever action he thought was appropriate. To be sure, there are a variety of ways to do so without being required to use the same words over and over.

In cases alleging excessive force, officers should expect to know and understand the seminal case of *Graham v. Connor*. While the vast majority of police officers comprehend that *Graham* requires that an officer's use of force is to be judged using the "objective reasonableness" standard, many officers may not know what that test actually requires. For example, Graham dictates that in determining the objective reasonableness of the officer's use of force, one must take into consideration the "tense, uncertain, and rapidly evolving" circumstances that the officer was confronted with at the time the purported unlawful force was used. Thus, prior to giving his testimony the officer will be reminded that when he relates the facts surrounding the arrest, he must incorporate these key issues. Again, this does not necessarily mean that the officer must use the precise words of "tense" or "rapidly evolving" throughout his testimony. Surely, by describing the events with these words in mind, however, the testimony will naturally weave in similar words that will certainly aid in painting a much more vivid picture of how quickly the events unfolded, an issue that is all too common in claims involving allegations of excessive force.

Officers who understand the defense theory will also be prepared to field questions from the plaintiff's attorney that may be unexpected. No doubt, experienced police defense attorneys can generally anticipate the vast majority of questions the plaintiff's attorney will ask and, therefore, will be able to prepare the officer for the appropriate responses. However, they cannot predict them all. Yet, if the officer is well prepared on the theory of the defense, he will nonetheless be able to adequately respond to the question, even if it does come out of left field.

Before providing testimony, the officer should appreciate the different roles of the attorneys that may question him in depositions or at trial. For example, an attorney representing the plaintiff—the person suing the officer—is entitled to ask leading questions during cross-examination. These types of questions typically leave no room for explanation. Instead, they require a "yes" or "no" answer.

Of course, it is a natural reaction for any officer to attempt to offer an explanation, but a savvy plaintiff's attorney, particularly at trial, will shut the officer down by asking the court to strike the officer's explanation and/or to admonish the officer to only answer the question with a "yes" or "no" response. And, if an officer is not prepared to expect this, he may fall into a trap where he continues to try to offer explanations only to be continually shut down. And if he is not careful, he may appear frustrated and angry before a jury. And that is exactly what the plaintiff's attorney wants. After all, if an officer appears frustrated and angry after being asked questions in a courtroom, jurors may be left wondering how the officer might have reacted out on the street under more stressful conditions.

On the other hand, a properly prepared officer will know to expect this type of questioning and that he should respond calmly and professionally. He will also know that after the plaintiff's attorney finishes, the officer's defense attorney will bring the officer "back" to the question that required some sort of explanation as follows: "Now officer, when Mr. Plaintiff's Attorney asked you this, and you responded by saying that, what did you mean when you said that?" This allows the officer to direct his attention to the jurors and offer the explanation and, in the process, educate the jurors as to why he did what he did (hopefully by incorporating for example, in an excessive force case, that the situation was escalating, that it was unknown whether the plaintiff/offender had any weapons, and a crowd was starting to develop around him and other officers. See how easy it can be to weave in the "tense, uncertain, and rapidly evolving" aspect of *Graham?*). Because the officer is prepared to expect leading questions from the plaintiff's attorney, the chances are less likely that he will come across as being defensive. Why is that so important? Because just like officers, jurors think that only a guilty person, or a person with something to hide, acts defensively.

Finally, a police officer accused of violating a plaintiff's civil rights must understand the role that he plays in testifying. While it is true that the officer's primary role is to explain the reasons he took certain actions through his testimony, the most important aspect of the officer's testimony is the *manner* in which he testifies.

Obviously, a properly prepared officer will have practiced answering questions. During that process, officers should expect their defense attorney to play the role of devil's advocate. At some point during the preparation process, the officer's attorney may say to the officer, "You know, I've been thinking about your testimony, and I have to tell you, I'm not sure this makes any sense," or ask "Are you sure?" or something similar. The objective is to first see how the officer reacts to such a question. If he becomes defensive, the attorney has a pretty good idea that the officer will probably react that way on tough cross-examination from the plaintiff's attorney. If that is the case, much of the preparation will be spent practicing how to properly and professionally respond to those tough questions.

Additionally, defendant police officers will be advised to take on the role of a teacher while they are on the witness stand as many potential jurors have a distorted view of what police work really entails. Police officers should not assume that jurors understand what law enforcement officers do. Indeed, many of today's potential jurors are used to seeing crime shows like "Law and Order," "CSI" and others, and, therefore, they have no idea what the job of a police officer really encompasses. As such, police officers have an obligation, if they want to assist in their defense, to inform the jurors of what that job demands.

Additionally, when officers take on the role of educators, they will naturally come across less defensive. They're forced to look at the jurors directly. Think about your own school days—can you recall any teacher or professor failing to look at the class while he or she taught an hour-long lesson? Probably not. And by making eye contact with the jurors, it makes the officer appear more human, professional and friendly. And *that's* precisely what the police defense attorney wants—to humanize the officer in front of a jury.

In sum, for their defense to be successful, police officers must understand the defense theory, the role of the opposing attorneys, and the role that they, themselves, play in the civil rights litigation. Law enforcement officers are not handed firearms and badges without being properly trained regarding the laws of search and seizure, the proper techniques in detaining or arresting citizens, and methods for dealing with members of the general public. Why then, would police officers be expected to know how to properly testify when they are the subject of a civil rights lawsuit without adequate preparation and training?

Laura L. Scarry is a partner in the law firm of DeAno & Scarry with offices located in Chicago and Wheaton, IL. Her practice focuses on the defense of police officers, police administrators and their agencies in civil rights litigation in state and federal court. She is also a former police officer with the City of Lake Forest, IL. She can be reached at lscarry@www.deanoandscarry.com.

USING FORENSIC EQUIPMENT TO ENHANCE USE OF FORCE INVESTIGATIONS

by Curtis J. (Jeff) Cope and Kim Swobodzinski

The clock struck 9 a.m. as the Magistrate, The Honorable John Q Jones, entered the courtroom and took his place on the large Mahogany bench, where he presides. The flags of the State and the United States of America are proudly displayed behind him. His footsteps could be heard to the rear of the courtroom through the silence as he slowly walked to take his place on the bench. He swiftly looked around the Courtroom at both sides of the bench and the packed audience that sat quietly and solemnly as they anxiously awaited him taking the bench.

The Court Bailiff rose and with a deep echoing voice stated the District Court, of the United States of America, will now come to order. The Honorable John Q Jones presiding. As everyone took their seats, the nervousness and squeamishness could be felt throughout the courtroom. It was a packed courtroom of viewers filled and fueled with mixed emotions, friends and family from both sides of the tables, all anxiously awaiting the opening statements of both sides. The Media, anxiously jotting their opening lines for their five o'clock reports could be heard through the silence.

His Honor picked up the Case File and began to read the charges aloud. Counselor, he stated, your clients are charged with Assault with a Deadly Weapon with Great Bodily Injury, Assault under Color of Authority, Violation of Civil Rights. Do your clients understand the charges that have been brought against them? Yes, the private attorney replied. How then, the Magistrate replied, do these Defendants wish to proceed?

Obviously, the situation described above is a horror story for any law enforcement officer, but one that is happening far too often in today's world.

So what can individual officers or departments do to protect themselves from being placed into this courtroom/use of force scenario? We would suggest what might appear to be a simple, yet effective solution that would involve by following some simple protocol steps, whenever an officer is involved in a use of force situation. These steps can help document how the incident occurred, and help protect the evidence that will assist in being successful in prosecuting the offender as well as providing necessary and useful evidence for a civil litigation later down the road.

Legal Justification for Contacting the Subject

One of the requirements for any contact with a citizen is having legal bases for the contact. It is understood that a law enforcement officer can engage anyone in a consensual encounter contact. There is no legal requirement for an officer to walk up to someone and begin talking to him or her. Where this changes is when the officer develops reasonable suspicion to take the encounter into a custodial detention or the officer develops probable cause to make an arrest.

This will also hold true when the citizen encounter starts with reasonable suspicion to detain or probable cause to arrest is present at the onset of the encounter.

Being able to write in a logical sequence, a written scenario that fully describes what happens during a law enforcement contact is a mandate for today's law enforcement officer. Law enforcement officers need to understand and be able to articulate why they are contacting an individual. Being able to write and describe all of the activity leading up to the contact in a police report is a crucial first step. Officers need to write out detailed and descriptive word images, which will describe the events leading up to a contact, so it is clear to the reader exactly what happened throughout the incident. If the contact escalates into a use of force, the need for complete documentation becomes more crucial. It is incumbent for the officer to report the type of force used, the reasons for its application, the effectiveness or ineffectiveness of the force option on the suspect and all after action steps taken. These written documents should allow the reader to imagine or picture in their mind all of the events that are unfolding.

Once the use of force is over and the suspect is taken into custody the officer or responding supervisor should consider using other forensic tools to help document, enhance and aid in making the word picture come alive. So what tools should the officer consider and why?

Camera

The use of a film-based or digital camera will assist in capturing in detail the vivid images of how the incident unfolded, the amount of force used during the incident, officer's/suspect/witness perspectives throughout the incident, after action results, physical injuries to the parties involved (both officer and suspect), damage to property, clothing, equipment, etc., and reflect what was seen by the parties involved as closely to real time and conditions as possible. The selection of a still or video camera will depend on what is being depicted, documented and department policy. Video cameras are excellent for documenting the overall scene of an incident. This type of camera also can be used to document and record witness statements, physical evidence, surroundings of the incident scene, weather and lighting conditions, etc. The still camera can also be used for all of the above but has limitations when it comes to getting sound bites from witnesses. The still camera is usually better for documenting evidence up-close or evidence that is small. It is also easier to use and usually has less of a learning curve for the operator compared to a high-tech video unit.

Digital still cameras are more costly than comparable film-based cameras, but they do not incur recurring costs of film and processing, and they generally have higher capacities than film-based cameras. The extra expense is quickly recovered by not having to buy consumables such as film and processing chemicals. In some cases, a digital camera will be able to record hundreds of images before its internal memory is full. This encourages the investigator to take lots of photographs without the concern of increasing costs due to film and processing, or simply running out of film in the field. The digital images can be preserved by downloading them to a department server, or "burning" them onto an inexpensive (and non-erasable) compact disk.

When using these types of tools, pay attention to detail. Use the devices to substantiate or discount what interviews or written documents have revealed. If the officer has said that he struck the suspect in the leg with a side handle baton, photographs could tell you whether it is true or not, direction of travel of the strikes and the implement used to deliver the blows. See Figure One. You can also tell the differences of the implement used. See Figure Two. This photograph demonstrates the difference bruise patterns between a side-handle baton as compared to a collapsing metal style baton.

If the use of force has been applied against the officer the use of these devices can assist to demonstrate the effects of incoming fire. They could be used to determine that an officer's response to this type of attack was objectively reasonable. See Figure Three. This photograph demonstrates the use of rods to enhance the view of the path and number of the bullets fired at the police unit.

What if the suspect claims that the officer has used excessive force when taking him or her into custody? Using photographic evidence can assist in determining whether the suspect is telling the truth or discount their claims. See Figure Four. This bruise pattern was claimed to have been caused by handcuffs being applied too tightly. The patterns themselves are not consistent with typical handcuff bruise patterns. See Figure Five. This is the view of the bruise patterns, on the same forearm as figure four, from a different angle.

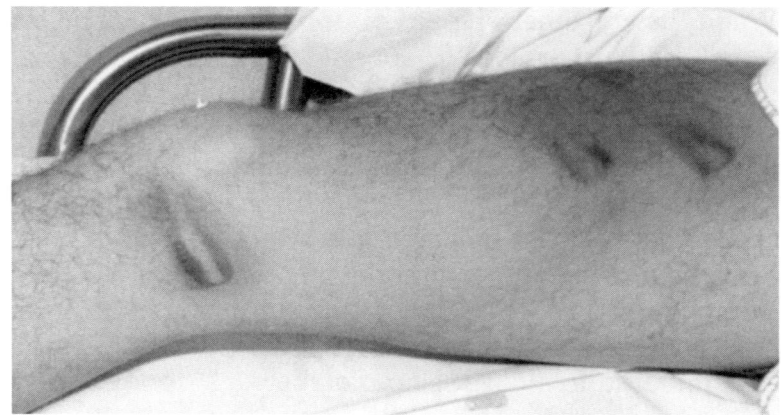

Figure One: These demonstrate classic side-handle baton strike bruise patterns. These are recognizable by the well-defined valley between the two red marks. The strike direction of travel of can usually be determined by where the heavy blood concentration is located.

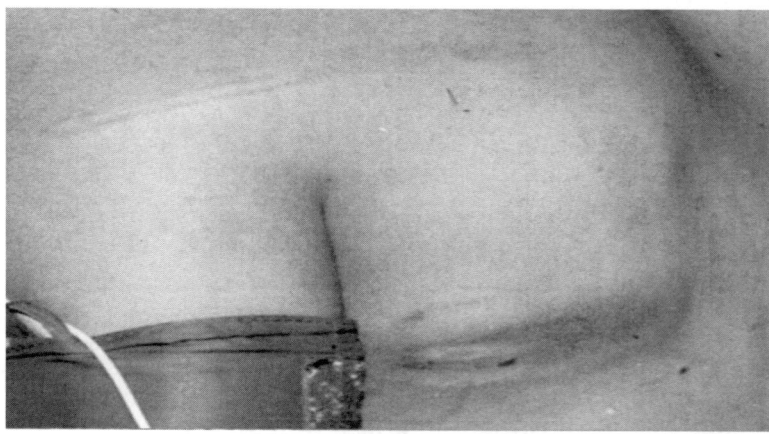

Figure Two: The collapsing metal baton bruise pattern is located at the top portion of the photograph. The thin valley between the parallel lines distinguishes the type of instrument. The small darker bruise closer to the top middle suggests that the small tip of the baton landed there. Contrast this to the much larger side handled baton strike below it.

Figure Three: The rods inserted into bullet holes can enhance the visual effect as well as demonstrate how effective they might be.

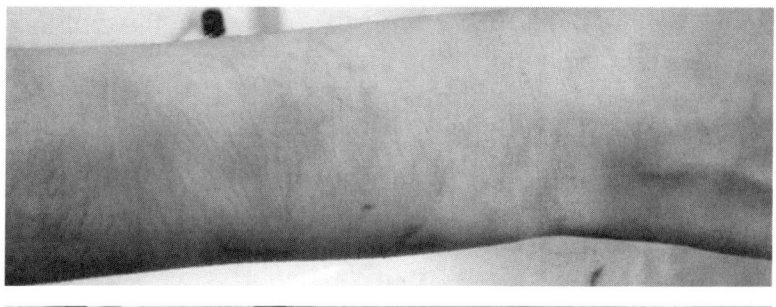

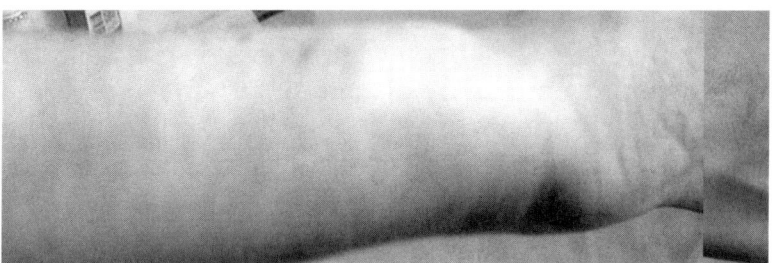

Figure Four and Five: These markings represent injuries that were claimed to have been caused by applying handcuffs too tightly. It is clear from these patterns that they were not classic handcuff bruise patterns. They also demonstrated that the markings were not consistent with where police officers are taught to apply handcuffs.

Suggested positions for the camera are as follows:

- Overall view of the incident site, surrounding area, lighting, footing and crowd at the time of the incident. Consideration should also be given to the tactical aspects of the scene that deal with officer safety issues.
- Aerial photographs of the incident site
- Positioning of where officers, suspects and witnesses were at the beginning of the incident
- Positioning changes of the above during the incident
- Overall views of the suspect, which should document any injury or the lack of injury.
- Overall views of the officers, in uniform or the clothing worn at the time of the incident, which should show any injury or damage to the officer and the officer's uniform or equipment
- Close-up shots of specific injury site, both with and without a measuring device, such as a ruler.
- Close-up shots of specific evidence
- Bruise patterns or markings that are claimed to have been caused by the use of force
- Locations on the body where the suspect claims to have been struck by officers but there is no visible evidence to support the claim. This could also be reversed and applied to an officer who claims to have been struck by the suspect but there is no visible evidence to support the claim.

Audio Recording Devices

There is a growing trend to provide law enforcement officers with some means of carrying audio recording devices while the officer is on-duty. With the advances in technology and dropping costs, providing recording devices for officers makes good sense. Many agencies are requiring officers to record all contacts, citizen or suspects alike, which the officer contacts during any official action. This type of action again makes good sense. Agencies with this type of policy are finding that officer's reports are more thorough and complete, scenes are described better, reports are being completed faster, citizen complaints are reduced and officers are accepting devices as a good tool. One of the many benefits with using digital (as opposed to tape-based) audio recording devices is that the recordings can be downloaded into the organizations computer servers. Once that is accomplished, the contents can be included in investigations that aid in prosecution. Witness statements are locked in at the time that they gave them, which is in fact when their memories are freshest.

These statements can be especially useful in use of force investigations. Getting statements from witnesses, suspects and officers alike can be helpful in determining what happened before, during and after the use of force. It is helpful if the person recording the information can identify who is speaking, where that person was during the incident as well as what they saw. In many cases, persons have been quoted in an official report as saying specific things, only to recant later on in an investigation. It is difficult for that person to explain why they stated something one way, which was recorded, and have later changed their rendition of the events.

When officers are wearing recording devices and become involved in a use of force, actual conversations, orders, suspect's responses, etc., get recorded. In the vast majority of cases, the officers resort to their training and do not concern themselves with the fact that they are wearing a recording device. When the recordings are reviewed it is found that suspects are being given lawful orders to comply and they are refusing to do so. In many incidents it can be heard that officers are telling suspects to quit fighting and submit to custody. These utterances are powerful when produced in court actions to demonstrate the officer's reasonableness in using force.

Selection of a device is dependant upon what best suits the needs of the person wearing it. Voice activated models seem to make the most sense for law enforcement. Some examples of what the devices should contain include the ability to be worn in a pocket or belt case. They must be rugged to stand up to the daily routine of law enforcement. Replaceable batteries still are used in some models but more and more are of the type that are rechargeable. Rechargeable batteries save on recurring costs, but they don't have the capacity of replaceable batteries, and if they run down unexpectedly, the device is useless. Replaceable batteries can be purchased nearly anywhere, and spares are east to carry when they do run down.

The decision to use a model that has the micro cassette tapes versus one that has a memory card makes the difference in price and usability. Tapes have to be replaced and cannot be downloaded without special adaptors. A tape might also contain recordings of multiple incidents, making it difficult to preserve the original recording without compromising its integrity. It is also easy to record over a previous recording without realizing that you are doing so when using a tape-based recorder. Digital models usually save recordings as separate files that are erased only on command, making inadvertent erasure less likely, and a digital copy of a recording is identical to the original. Tape-based recordings are usually analog, and degrade with each generation of copy. Memory cards come in a variety of capacities, the larger sizes providing more recording time, and the cards last indefinitely. Many models are capable of recording for 20 or more hours without overwhelming the memory card. The ability to download to a computer is a <u>must</u> feature. Cost can be as low as $65.00 for one that could fit the need. Obviously the higher the cost the more you get for your investment.

Other Technology Advances

Using a computer to recreate incidents is becoming more commonplace in use of force investigations. Animated reenactments of incidents can be accomplished by using tools that are common in computers today. Using these tools takes some special computer skills but the end result can have a dramatic effect on a jury when they can see what actually happened in the incident. Actual photographic evidence, from the scene, can be used to enhance the presentations. Some additional advantages of using animated recreations are that you can demonstrate what the officer saw from his perspective or that of the suspect or witness. Actual timing sequences can be built into the production as well as distance covered, direction of travel, body dynamics, flight paths of objects or rounds fired, etc. Great strides are being made in this area at the Force Science Research Center, a Non-profit institution based at Minnesota State University, Mankato, Minnesota. Readers can find out more about this Institute by logging onto their web site at www.forcesciencenews.com.

Other computer programs allow for photographs to be inserted in a 360-degree format and from each person's perspective. The computer program allows for the program operator to place hot buttons into the production, so that by clicking onto the button moves the view to that location. The program then shows what can be viewed from that perspective. By placing where the officer, suspect and witnesses were at the time of the incident the program gives their view of the scene. These views can be moved just like during the incident simulating the dynamics of the use of force.

The Bottom Line

Writing excellent police reports is something that officers should strive for whenever they write any written products. The police officer's written report used to be all one would need to be successful in prosecuting a suspect when a use of force had been alleged. More and more today, the expectation is to have forensic evidence to support what has been claimed in writing. To use forensic equipment takes additional time and resources but the end result is well worth the investment.

Curtis J. (Jeff) Cope was a 29½-year veteran police officer. He retired from active service in late 1997 as a lieutenant in charge of General Investigation Bureau at Huntington Beach, CA. Police Department. He is a federal and state court-recognized expert in use of force, police practices, supervision issues, training and an instructor in defense tactics/arrest and control techniques, force investigations. He is also a certified Master Instructor by the California Commission on Peace Officers Standards and Training (P.O.S.T.).

He is now a private Consultant and is the Program Administrator of the P.O.S.T. Robert Presley Institution of Criminal Investigation, Instructor Development Workshop course.

He can be reached at curtisjcope@mindspring.com, www.curtisjcope.com or 714-962-1931.

Kimberle Swobodzinski is currently an Identification Technician with the Gardena, California Police Department. She has been working crime scene investigations for the past sixteen and a half years. She has testified as expert witness in crime scene investigations and homicide investigations. She assists in teaching Crime Scene Management Training Blocks for the L.A.P.D. Institute of Criminal Investigation Core Courses and is a graduate of the POST Master Instructor Development Program. She can be reached at Swobodzinski@gardenapd.org.